SHORT STORY WRITERS AND SHORT STORIES

BLOOM'S LITERARY CRITICISM 20TH ANNIVERSARY COLLECTION

BLOOM'S LITERARY CRITICISM **20**TH **ANNIVERSARY COLLECTION**

Dramatists and Dramas
The Epic
Essayists and Prophets
Novelists and Novels
Poets and Poems
Short Story Writers and Short Stories

SHORT STORY WRITERS AND SHORT STORIES

BLOOM'S LITERARY CRITICISM 20TH ANNIVERSARY COLLECTION

Harold Bloom

Sterling Professor of the Humanities
Yale University

CHELSEA HOUSE
PUBLISHERS

A Haights Cross Communications ⚡ Company ®

Philadelphia

Library of Congress Cataloging-in-Publication Data

Bloom, Harold.
  Short story writers and short stories / Harold Bloom.
    p. cm. — (Bloom's 20th anniversary collection)
  ISBN 0-7910-8228-8 HC 0-7910-8367-5 PB
  1. Short story. I. Title.
  PN3373.B57 2005
  808.83'1—dc22

                                    2005006399

Cover designed by Takeshi Takahashi
Cover illustration by David Levine
Layout by EJB Publishing Services

Table of Contents

Preface

Harold Bloom

I BEGAN EDITING ANTHOLOGIES OF LITERARY CRITICISM FOR CHELSEA House in early 1984, but the first volume, *Edgar Allan Poe: Modern Critical Views*, was published in January, 1985, so this is the twentieth anniversary of a somewhat Quixotic venture. If asked how many separate books have been issued in this project, I no longer have a precise answer, since in so long a span many volumes go out of print, and even whole series have been discontinued. A rough guess would be more than a thousand individual anthologies, a perhaps insane panoply to have been collected and introduced by a single critic.

Some of these books have surfaced in unlikely places: hotel rooms in Bologna and Valencia, Coimbra and Oslo; used-book stalls in Frankfurt and Nice; on the shelves of writers wherever I have gone. A batch were sent by me in answer to a request from a university library in Macedonia, and I have donated some of them, also by request, to a number of prisoners serving life sentences in American jails. A thousand books across a score of years can touch many shores and many lives, and at seventy-four I am a little bewildered at the strangeness of the endeavor, particularly now that it has leaped between centuries.

It cannot be said that I have endorsed every critical essay reprinted, as my editor's notes have made clear. Yet the books have to be reasonably reflective of current critical modes and educational fashions, not all of them provoking my own enthusiasm. But then I am a dinosaur, cheerfully naming myself as "Bloom Brontosaurus Bardolator." I accept only three criteria for greatness in imaginative literature: aesthetic splendor, cognitive power, wisdom. What is now called "relevance" will be in the dustbins in less than a generation, as our society (somewhat tardily) reforms prejudices and inequities. The fashionable in literature and criticism always ebbs away into Period Pieces. Old, well-made furniture survives as valuable antiques, which is not the destiny of badly constructed imaginings and ideological exhortings.

Time, which decays and then destroys us, is even more merciless in obliterating weak novels, poems, dramas, and stories, however virtuous these may be. Wander into a library and regard the masterpieces of thirty years ago: a handful of forgotten books have value, but the iniquity of oblivion has rendered most bestsellers instances of time's revenges. The other day a friend and former student told me that the first of the Poets Laureate of twentieth-century America had been Joseph Auslander, concerning whom even my still retentive memory is vacant. These days, Mrs. Felecia Hemans is studied and taught by a number of feminist Romantic scholars. Of the poems of that courageous wisdom, who wrote to support her brood, I remember only the opening line of "Casabianca" but only because Mark Twain added one of his very own to form a couplet:

The boy stood on the burning deck
Eating peanuts by the peck.

Nevertheless, I do not seek to affirm the social inutility of literature, though I admire Oscar Wilde's grand declaration: "All art is perfectly useless." Shakespeare may well stand here for the largest benign effect of the highest literature: properly appreciated, it can heal part of the violence that is built into every society whatsoever. In my own judgment, Walt Whitman is the central writer yet brought forth by the Americas—North, Central, South, Caribbean—whether in English, Spanish, Portuguese, French, Yiddish or other tongues. And Walt Whitman is a healer, a poet-prophet who discovered his pragmatic vocation by serving as a volunteer, unpaid wound-dresser and nurse in the Civil War hospitals of Washington, D.C. To read and properly understand Whitman can be an education in self-reliance and in the cure of your own consciousness.

The function of literary criticism, as I conceive it in my gathering old age, is primarily appreciation, in Walter Pater's sense, which fuses analysis and evaluation. When Pater spoke of "art for art's sake' he included in the undersong of his declaration what D.H. Lawrence meant by "art for life's sake," Lawrence, the most provocative of post-Whitmanian vitalists, has now suffered a total eclipse in the higher education of the English-speaking nations. Feminists have outlawed him with their accusations of misogyny, and they describe him as desiring women to renounce sexual pleasure. On this supposed basis, students lose the experience of reading one of the major authors of the twentieth century, at once an unique novelist, story-teller, poet, critic, and prophet.

An enterprise as vast as Chelsea House Literary Criticism doubtless reflects both the flaws and the virtues of its editor. Comprehensiveness has been a goal throughout, and I have (for the most part) attempted to set aside many of my own literary opinions. I sorrow when the market keeps an important volume out of print, though I am solaced by the example of my idol, Dr. Samuel Johnson, in his *Lives of the Poets*. The booksellers (who were both publishers and retailers) chose the poets, and Johnson was able to say exactly what he thought of each. Who remembers such worthies as Yalden, Sprat, Roscommon, and Stepney? It would be invidious for me to name the contemporary equivalents, but their name is legion.

I have been more fully educated by this quest for comprehensivness, which taught me how to write for a larger audience. Literary criticism is both an individual and communal mode. It has its titans: Johnson, Coleridge, Lessing, Goethe, Hazlitt, Sainte-Beuve, Pater, Curtius, Valèry, Frye, Empson, Kenneth Burke are among them. But most of those I reprint cannot be of that eminence: one makes a heap of all that can be found. Over a lifetime in reading and teaching one learns so much from so many that no one can be certain of her or his intellectual debts. Hundreds of those I have reprinted I never will meet, but they have helped enlighten me, insofar as I have been capable of learning from a host of other minds.

Introduction

Harold Bloom

THOUGH THERE ARE COMMENTARIES HERE UPON THIRTY-NINE MASTERS OF the short story, I regret such absences as Alice Munro, Saki, Edna O'Brien, A.E. Coppard, Frank O'Connor, Katherine Mansfield and such earlier magnificences as E.T.A. Hoffmann, Kleist, Tolstoy, Leskov, Hardy—among many others.

Frank O'Connor wrote a provocative study of the short story, *The Lonely Voice* (1963), which still moves me to useful disagreement. It always puzzles me that O'Connor was marvelous on Shakespeare, yet *The Lonely Voice* is nowhere close to the distinction of *Shakespeare's Progress*, one of the admirable *literary* studies of the greatest of all writers. Perhaps O'Connor was too close to the art of the short story, which he saw as the lonely voice of "submerged population groups." O'Connor somehow had to believe that:

> ... the short story remains by its very nature remote from the community—romantic, individualistic, and intransigent.

I can recognize D.H. Lawrence and James Joyce, Hemingway and Katherine Anne Porter by that description, but not Hans Christian Andersen, Turgenev, Mark Twain, Tolstoy, Kipling, Isaac Babel. Lyric poetry from the Renaissance through the Romantics on to W.B. Yeats emanates from a lovely tower, but short stories do not necessarily reflect any particular social dialectics.

The short story has no Homer or Shakespeare, Dickens or Proust: not even Turgenev nor Chekhov, Joyce nor Lawrence, Borges nor Kafka, Flannery O'Connor nor Edna O'Brien can be said to dominate the form. If I hear someone name the genre of the epic, I think first of Homer or of Milton, and almost anyone responds to a mention of verse-drama with

Hamlet. Is it merely a personal peculiarity that short stories evoke in me an immediate sense of multiplicity, whereas lyric poems suggest Shelley and Keats? Is there something more anonymous about the short story as a form? Frank O'Connor would reject my question: individualism and intransigence hardly cohere with anonymity. I suspect that there are generic elements that bind together short stories more closely than do the common features of poems, plays, and novels.

And yet if I brood upon some of my favorite storytellers of the twentieth century, say Henry James and D.H. Lawrence, I have little sense that they are composing in the same genre: Lawrence's extraordinary vitalism is expressionistic; James's nuances are impressionistic. Frank O'Connor, true to his critical obsession, diagnoses Lawrence as "running away from the submerged population among which he grew up", but I think that is a reduction of Lawrence's drive to get out of our naturally fallen condition, our "crucifixion into sex", as he put it. James stays in the world of his upbringing, while mixing sexuality and ghostliness into a fascinating compound. What then, as story writers, did Lawrence and James possess in common?

Lawrence, as a storyteller, derived from Thomas Hardy, while James blent together Turgenev and Hawthorne. Yet neither Lawrence nor James was a fantasist, in the mode that includes H.C. Andersen, Poe, Gogol, Lewis Carroll, Kafka, and Borges. If the primary tradition of the short story is Chekhovian, the alternate mode is Kafkan-Borgesian, nightmare phantasmagorias. Lawrence and James have recognizable qualities that are Chekhovian, and neither were precursors of Borges.

Frank O'Connor thought of the short story as a Chekhovian art, crowded by a "new submerged population of doctors, teachers, and sometimes priests". Yet in reading Chekhov I have the impression that everyone is submerged, by loneliness and by misunderstanding. Chiding Kipling for having too much of a sense of the group, O'Connor seems to me scarcely coherent. Must a short story be about human loneliness if it is to endure?

Mark Twain, Thomas Mann, Hemingway, Faulkner, and Scott Fitzgerald all knew a great deal about loneliness, but that hardly seems to me the center of any one of them as a tale-teller. Lawrence told us to trust the tale, not the artist, and great stories rarely manifest only a single human characteristic. I wonder which is my favorite among all the stories commented upon in this volume? Is it Babel's "How It Was Done in Odessa" or Hans Christian Andersen's "Auntie Toothache"? Babel's Benya Krik and the demoness Auntie Toothache are anything but submerged voices. Perhaps short stories are allied to one another only as miracles.

Alexandr Pushkin

(1799-1837)

OF THE PROSE TALES OF PUSHKIN, THE MOST POWERFUL (IN TRANSLATION) is clearly the novella *The Queen of Spades*, though the fuller length of *The Captain's Daughter* does reveal some of Pushkin's more varied narrative resources. Paul Debreczeny has culminated a Russian critical tradition of reading *The Queen of Spades* as a Kabbalistic parable, and to Debreczeny's intricate unpacking of the story's dense symbolism I desire to add nothing. But as a critical Kabbalist myself, I know that a Kabbalistic parable, whether in Pushkin or Kafka, shows us that rhetoric, cosmology, and psychology are not three subjects but three in one, and so I turn to the psychology of *The Queen of Spades*.

What is the secret misfortune that the Countess, Queen of Spades, signifies? Does Hermann frighten her to death, or does she pass on to him the curse of St. Germain and so only then is able to die? What we know most surely about the Countess is that she was, is, and will be rancid, a fit mistress for St. Germain (if that is what she was). What we know most surely about Hermann is that he is just as rancid, but unlike the Countess he is trapped in irony every time he speaks. His most extraordinary entrapments come in the first and last sentences we hear him speak: "The game fascinates me, but I am not in the position to sacrifice the essentials of life in the hope of acquiring the luxuries," and the insane, repetitious mutter, "Three, seven, ace! Three, seven, queen!" He of course does sacrifice the true essentials of life, and the identification of the Countess with the Queen of Spades or death-in-life ironically substitutes for the ace of occult success the Kabbalistic crown that is at once a pinnacle and the abyss of nothingness.

Psychologically Hermann and the Countess are very similar, each being compounded of worldly ambition and the diabolic, but the Countess

1

refuses to accept Hermann as her initiate until after she is dead. While alive, all that she will say to Hermann is "It was a joke." It is again a diabolic irony that Hermann answers, "There's no joking about it," since her final joke will render him insane, the joke being the Kabbalistic substitution of the Queen of Spades for the ace. Yet the Countess's apparition speaks in terms that cannot be reconciled with much in the story's overdetermined symbolism:

> "I have come to you against my will," she said in a firm voice, "but I have been ordered to fulfill your request. Three, seven, ace, played in that order, will win for you, but only on condition that you play not more than one card in twenty-four hours, and that you never play again for the rest of your life. I'll forgive you my death if you marry my ward, Lisaveta Ivanovna."

Is it St. Germain or the Devil himself, each presumably on the other side of life, who compels her to come? Whose is the lie, as to the last card, hers or a power beyond her? Why would she wish the horrible Hermann upon poor Lisaveta Ivanovna? Is it because she now cares for her ward, or is it malice towards all concerned? Why three days for the card game rather than one? I do not think that there are aesthetic answers to these questions. What matters, aesthetically, is that we are compelled to try to answer them, that we also are swept into this Kabbalistic narrative of compulsions, deceptions, betrayals, Napoleonic drives. Pushkin has created an overdetermined cosmos and placed us firmly within it, subject to the same frightening forces that his protagonists have to endure.

The trope that governs the cosmos of *The Queen of Spades* is Dantesque, purgatorial exile: "You shall learn the salt taste of another's bread, and the hard path up and down his stairs." That is Dante at Ravenna and Lisaveta Ivanovna in the house of the Countess, but those purgatorial stairs are ascended also by Hermann and the Countess, both to ill effect. The power of *The Queen of Spades* is both purgatorial and infernal, and the reader, who is exposed to both realms, herself or himself chooses the path of the parable, a narrow, winding stair up, or the madness of Hermann's descent, outwards and downwards into wintry night.

Nathaniel Hawthorne

(1804–1864)

HENRY JAMES'S *HAWTHORNE* WAS PUBLISHED IN DECEMBER 1879, IN London, in the English Men of Letters series. Unique among the thirty-nine volumes of that group, this was a critical study of an American by an American. Only Hawthorne seemed worthy of being an English man of letters, and only James seemed capable of being an American critic. Perhaps this context inhibited James, whose *Hawthorne* tends to be absurdly overpraised, or perhaps Hawthorne caused James to feel an anxiety that even George Eliot could not bring the self-exiled American to experience. Whatever the reason, James wrote a study that requires to be read between the lines, as here in its final paragraph:

> He was a beautiful, natural, original genius, and his life had been singularly exempt from worldly preoccupations and vulgar efforts. It had been as pure, as simple, as unsophisticated, as his work. He had lived primarily in his domestic affections, which were of the tenderest kind; and then—without eagerness, without pretension, but with a great deal of quiet devotion—in his charming art. His work will remain; it is too original and exquisite to pass away; among the men of imagination he will always have his niche. No one has had just that vision of life, and no one has had a literary form that more successfully expressed his vision. He was not a moralist, and he was not simply a poet. The moralists are weightier, denser, richer, in a sense; the poets are more purely inconclusive and irresponsible. He combined in a singular degree the spontaneity of the imagination with a haunting care for moral problems. Man's conscience was his theme, but he saw it in the

3

light of a creative fancy which added, out of its own substance, an interest, and, I may almost say, an importance.

Is *The Scarlet Letter* pure, simple, and unsophisticated? Is *The Marble Faun* a work neither moral nor poetic? Can we accurately assert that man's conscience, however lit by creative fancy, is Hawthorne's characteristic concern? James's vision of his American precursor is manifestly distorted by a need to misread creatively what may hover too close, indeed may shadow the narrative space that James requires for his own enterprise. In that space, something beyond shadowing troubles James. Isabel Archer has her clear affinities with Dorothea Brooke, yet her relation to Hester Prynne is even more familial, just as Millie Theale will have the lineage of *The Marble Faun*'s Hilda ineluctably marked upon her. James's representations of women are Hawthornian in ways subtly evasive yet finally unmistakable. Yet even this influence and its consequent ambivalences do not seem to be the prime unease that weakens James's *Hawthorne*. Rather, the critical monograph is more embarrassed than it can know by James's guilt at having abandoned the American destiny. Elsewhere, James wrote to some purpose about Emerson (though not so well as his brother William did), but in *Hawthorne* the figure of Emerson is unrecognizable and the dialectics of New England Transcendentalism are weakly abused:

A grapher of Hawthorne might well regret that his hero had not been more mixed up with the reforming and free-thinking class, so that he might find a pretext for writing a chapter upon the state of Boston society forty years ago. A needful warrant for such regret should be, properly, that the biographer's own personal reminiscences should stretch back to that period and to the persons who animated it. This would be a guarantee of fulness of knowledge and, presumably, of kindness of tone. It is difficult to see, indeed, how the generation of which Hawthorne has given us, in *Blithedale*, a few portraits, should not, at this time of day, be spoken of very tenderly and sympathetically. If irony enter into the allusion, it should be of the lightest and gentlest. Certainly, for a brief and imperfect chronicler of these things, a writer just touching them as he passes, and who has not the advantage of having been a contemporary, there is only one possible tone. The compiler of these pages, though his recollections date only from a later period, has a memory of a certain number of persons who had been intimately connected, as Hawthorne was not, with the agitations of that interesting time. Something of its interest adhered to them still—something of its aroma clung to their garments; there was something about them which seemed to say that when they were young and enthusiastic, they had been initiated into moral mysteries, they had played at a wonderful game. Their usual mark (it is true I can think of exceptions) was that they seemed excellently good. They appeared unstained by the world, unfamiliar with worldly desires and standards, and with those various forms of human depravity which flourish in some high phases of civilisation; inclined to simple and democratic ways, destitute of pretensions and affectations, of jealousies, of cynicisms, of snobbishness. This little epoch of fermentation has three or four drawbacks for the critics—drawbacks, however, that may be overlooked by a person for whom it has an interest of association. It bore, intellectually, the stamp of provincialism; it was a beginning without a fruition, a dawn without a noon; and it produced, with a single exception, no great talents. It produced a great deal of writing, but (always putting Hawthorne aside, as a contemporary but not a sharer) only one writer in whom the world at large has interested itself. The situation was summed up and transfigured in the admirable and exquisite Emerson. He expressed all that it contained, and a good deal more, doubtless, besides; he was the man of genius of the moment; he was the Transcendentalist *par excellence*. Emerson expressed, before all things, as was extremely natural at the hour and in the place, the value and importance of the individual, the duty of making the most of one's self, of living by one's own personal light, and carrying out one's own disposition. He reflected with beautiful irony upon the exquisite impudence of those institutions which claim to have appropriated the truth and to dole it out, in proportionate morsels, in exchange for a subscription. He talked about the beauty and dignity of life, and about every one who is born into the world being born to the whole, having an interest and a stake in the whole. He said "all that is clearly due to-day is not to lie," and a great many other things which it would be still easier to present in a ridiculous light. He insisted upon sincerity and independence and spontaneity, upon acting in harmony with one's nature, and not conforming and compromising for the sake of being more comfortable. He urged that a man should await his call, his finding the thing to do which he should really believe in doing, and not be urged by the world's opinion to do simply the world's work. "If no call should come for years, for centuries, then I know that the want of the Universe is the attestation of faith by my abstinence.... If I cannot work, at least I need not lie." The doctrine of the supremacy of the individual to himself, of his originality, and, as regards his own character, *unique* quality, must have had a great charm for people living in a society in which introspection—thanks to the want of other entertainment—played almost the part of a social resource.

The "admirable and exquisite Emerson" was "as sweet as barbed wire," to quote President Giamatti of Yale. Any reader of that great, grim, and most American of books, *The Conduct of Life*, ought to have known this. James's Emerson, dismissed here by the novelist as a provincial of real charm, had provoked the senior Henry James to an outburst of more authentic critical value: "O you man without a handle!" Hawthorne too, in a very different way, was a man without a handle, not less conscious and subtle an artist than the younger Henry James himself. *The Scarlet Letter*, in James's *Hawthorne*, is rightly called the novelist's masterpiece, but then is accused of "a want of reality and an abuse of the fanciful element—of a certain superficial symbolism." James was too good a reader to have indicted Hawthorne for "a want of reality," were it not that Hawthornian representation had begun too well the process of causing a Jamesian aspect of reality to appear.

II

Hawthorne's highest achievement is not in *The Scarlet Letter* and *The Marble Faun*, distinguished as they are, but in the best of his tales and sketches. The last of these, the extraordinary "Feathertop," sub-titled "A Moralized Legend," is as uncanny a story as Kafka's "Country Doctor" or "Hunter Gracchus," and has about it the dark aura of Hawthorne's valediction, his farewell to his own art. In its extraordinary strength at representing an order of reality that intersects our own, neither identical with the mundane nor quite transcending the way things are, "Feathertop" may be without rivals in our language.

Mother Rigby, a formidable witch, sets out to create "as lifelike a scarecrow as ever was seen," and being weary of making hobgoblins, determines to give us "something fine, beautiful, and splendid." An authentic forerunner of Picasso as sculptor, the witch chooses her materials with bravura:

The most important item of all, probably, although it made so little show, was a certain broomstick, on which Mother Rigby had taken many an airy gallop at midnight, and which now served the scarecrow by way of a spinal column, or, as the unlearned phrase it, a backbone. One of its arms was a disabled flail, which used to be wielded by Goodman Rigby, before his spouse worried him out of this troublesome world; the other, if I mistake not, was composed of the pudding-stick and a broken rung of a chair, tied loosely together at the elbow. As for its legs, the right was a hoe-handle, and the left, an undistinguished and miscellaneous stick from the wood-pile. Its lungs, stomach, and other affairs of that kind, were nothing better than a meal-bag stuffed with straw. Thus, we have made out the skeleton and entire corporosity of the scarecrow, with the exception of its head; and this was admirably supplied by a somewhat withered and shrivelled pumpkin in which Mother Rigby cut two holes for the eyes and a slit for the mouth, leaving a bluish-colored knob, in the middle, to pass for a nose. It was really quite a respectable face.

Gaudily attired, the scarecrow so charms its demiurgic creator ("The more Mother Rigby looked, the better she was pleased") that she emulates Jehovah directly, and decides to breathe life into the new Adam by thrusting her own pipe into his mouth. Once vivified, Mother Rigby's creature is urged by her to emulate Milton's Adam: "Step forth! Thou hast the world before thee!" Hawthorne does not allow us to doubt the self-critique involved, as all romance is deliciously mocked:

In obedience to Mother Rigby's word, and extending its arm as if to reach her outstretched hand, the figure made a step forward—a kind of hitch and jerk, however, rather than a step—then tottered, and almost lost its balance. What could the witch expect? It was nothing, after all, but a scarecrow, stuck upon two sticks. But the strong-willed old beldam scowled, and beckoned, and flung the energy of her purpose so forcibly at this poor combination of rotten wood, and musty straw, and ragged garments, that it was compelled to show itself a man, in spite of the reality of things. So it stept into the bar of sunshine. There it stood—poor devil of a contrivance that it was!—with only the thinnest vesture of human similitude about it, through which was evident the stiff, ricketty, incongruous, faded, tattered, good-for-nothing patchwork of its substance, ready to sink in a heap upon the floor, as conscious of its own unworthiness to be erect. Shall I confess the truth? At its present point of vivification, the scarecrow reminds me of some of the lukewarm and abortive characters, composed of heterogeneous materials, used for the thousandth time, and never worth using, with which romance-writers (and myself, no doubt, among the rest) have so over-peopled the world of fiction.

But the critique surpasses mere writers and attacks the greatest of romancers, Jehovah himself, as Mother Rigby deliberately frightens her pathetic creature into speech. Now fully humanized, he is named Feathertop by his creator, endowed with wealth, and sent forth into the world to woo the beautiful Polly, daughter of the worshipful Judge Gookin. There is only the one catch; poor Feathertop must keep puffing at his pipe, or he will dwindle again to the elements that compose him. All goes splendidly; Feathertop is a social triumph, and well along to seducing the delicious Polly, when he is betrayed by glances in a mirror:

By and by, Feathertop paused, and throwing himself into an imposing attitude, seemed to summon the fair girl to survey his figure, and resist him longer, if she could. His star, his embroidery, his buckles, glowed, at that instant, with unutterable splendor; the picturesque hues of his attire took a richer depth of coloring; there was a gleam and polish over his whole presence, betokening the perfect witchery of well-ordered manners. The maiden raised her eyes, and suffered them to linger upon her companion with a bashful and admiring gaze. Then, as if desirous of judging what value her own simple comeliness might have, side by side with so much brilliancy, she cast a glance towards the full-length looking-glass, in front of which they happened to be standing. It was one of the truest plates in the world, and incapable of flattery. No sooner did the images, therein reflected, meet Polly's eye, than she shrieked, shrank from the stranger's side, gazed at him, for a moment, in the wildest dismay, and sank insensible upon the floor. Feathertop, likewise, had looked towards the mirror, and there beheld, not the glittering mockery of his outside show, but a picture of the sordid patchwork of his real composition, stript of all witchcraft.

Fleeing back to his mother, Feathertop abandons existence in despair of his reality, and flings the pipe away in a kind of suicide. His epitaph is spoken by a curiously softened Mother Rigby, as though experience had rendered her a more maternal demiurge:

> "Poor Feathertop!" she continued. "I could easily give him another chance, and send him forth again to-morrow. But, no! his feelings are too tender; his sensibilities too deep. He seems to have too much heart to bustle for his own advantage, in such an empty and heartless world. Well, well! I'll make a scarecrow of him, after all. 'Tis an innocent and a useful vocation, and will suit my darling well; and if each of his human brethren had as fit a one, 'twould be the better for mankind; and as for this pipe of tobacco, I need it more than he!"

Gentle and whimsical as this is, it may be Hawthorne's darkest irony. The witch is more merciful than the remorseless Jehovah, who always does send us forth again, into a world that cannot sustain us. Feathertop is closer to most of us than we are to Hester Prynne. That final dismissal of heroism is Hawthorne's ultimate legacy, glowing on still in the romances of Nathanael West and Thomas Pynchon.

III

There is no single way to characterize Nathaniel Hawthorne's complex vision of the American self. I think I have learned some of the intricacies of the Emersonian self in the Sage of Concord's work, and in its further developments (and departures) in Thoreau, Whitman, Dickinson, and Melville, all of whom would have been very different had Emerson never existed. Hawthorne's relationship to Emerson is far more difficult to perceive and describe. They were unlikely but fairly frequent walking-companions, with the essayist probably carrying most of the desultory discourse along. Except for his wife Lidian and daughter Ellen, Emerson really needed no one, though he found the taciturn Hawthorne pleasant enough company, if of little interest as a writer. But then, our national sage did not much enjoy prose fiction. The *Moralia* of Plutarch, Montaigne's essays, Dante and Shakespeare were Emerson's preferred reading. He searched for wit and wisdom, not for moral perplexity. Right and wrong were unambiguous for the prophet of self-reliance, at home with the God within, the best and oldest part of his being. Hawthorne, uneasy with Emerson, nevertheless could never quite evade him. Hester Prynne, like

Henry James's Isabel Archer, is the American Eve, and both are Emersonian, even as Whitman and Thoreau are versions of Emerson's American Adam, always early in the morning. Emerson, satirized by a defensive Melville in *Pierre* and in *The Confidence Man*, nevertheless is the American Plato who informs the Gnostic cosmos of *Moby Dick*, despite itself as profoundly Emerson as is the original 1855 *Leaves of Grass*. Captain Ahab refuses a role as American Adam, but his Promethean rebellion against the Creation-Fall of his catastrophic maiming by the snowy Leviathan allies him to the grim sublimity of Emerson's masterwork, *The Conduct of Life*. Hawthorne, of all the titans of the American Renaissance, has the subtlest and most surprising relationship to the inescapable Emersonian self.

"Young Goodman Brown" (1835) is early Hawthorne, composed when he was about thirty, and just beginning to fully find his mode as a writer. Poor Brown is not at all self-reliant, but a rather pathetic instance of societal over-conditioning. Hawthorne neither wants to be or is an Emersonian, yet he gives us a young "goodman" who badly needs a blood-transfusion from Hester Prynne, or some other fictive apostle of Emerson. One of many implicit Hawthornian ironies is that the strong self's cost of confirmation comes too high, while society's conformities are hopelessly low, and are not worth even the smallest price. Hawthorne never satirizes Emersonianism, because he agrees with its dialectic of self-reliance against societal repression, but he also shudders at Emerson's casual stance towards antinomianism. Still, Hawthorne has made his choice: he will not join Emerson's Party of Hope, but he has no use whatever for the Party of Memory. Like his more capable readers, Hawthone falls in love with Hester Prynne, and consigns the wretched Brown to a silent death-in-life:

> Had Goodman Brown fallen asleep in the forest, and only dreamed a wild dream of a witch-meeting?
>
> Be it so, if you will. But, alas! it was a dream of evil omen for young Goodman Brown. A stern, a sad, a darkly meditative, a distrustful, if not a desperate man, did he become, from the night of that fearful dream. On the Sabbath-day, when the congregation were singing a holy psalm, he could not listen, because an anthem of sin rushed loudly upon his ear, and drowned all the blessed strain. When the minister spoke from the pulpit, with power and fervid eloquence, and, with his hand on the open Bible, of the sacred truths of our religion, and of saint-like lives and triumphant deaths, and of future bliss or misery unutterable, then did Goodman Brown turn pale,

dreading, lest the roof should thunder down upon the gray blasphemer and his hearers. Often, awakening suddenly at midnight, he shrank from the bosom of Faith, and at morning or eventide, when the family knelt down at prayer, he scowled, and muttered to himself, and gazed sternly at his wife, and turned away. And when he had lived long, and was borne to his grave, a hoary corpse, followed by Faith, an aged woman, and his children and grand-children, a goodly procession, besides neighbors, not a few, they carved no hopeful verse upon his tomb-stone; for his dying hour was gloom.

Self-damnation could hardly go further, even in a tale by Hawthorne. What precisely has destroyed Brown? Is it the American Psychosis, as analyzed in a powerful essay of David Bromwich's (reprinted in this volume)? The living death of Brown would thus be another instance of the extinction of American radical Protestantism, the failed transformation of John Calvin to these shores. Jonathan Edwards is no longer even a ghostly presence, while Ralph Waldo Emerson lives on (except for the South). Perhaps Emerson is even too lively, since we are ruled by Emersonians of the Right, even as Emersonians of the Left go on destroying our universities in the name of sacred Resentment, determined to expiate, whatever it costs in humanistic culture. There are no young Goodman Browns among my current students, and only a few Hester Prynnes.

Hans Christian Andersen

(1805–1875)

ANDERSEN'S PRIME PRECURSORS WERE SHAKESPEARE AND SIR WALTER Scott, and his best work can be thought of as an amalgam of *A Midsummer Night's Dream* and the almost as magnificent "Wandering Willie's Tale" from Scott's *Redgauntlet*, with a certain admixture of Goethe and of the "Universal Romanticism" of Novalis and E.T.A. Hoffman. Goethean "renunciation" was central to Andersen's art, which truly worships only one god, who can be called Fate. Though Andersen was a grand original in his fairy tales, he eagerly accepted from folklore its stoic acceptance of fate. Nietzsche argued that, for the sake of life, origin and aim had to be kept apart. In Andersen, there was no desire to separate origin and aim. It cost his life much fulfillment: he never had a home of his own or a lasting love, but he achieved an extraordinary literary art.

Like Walt Whitman's, Andersen's authentic sexual orientation was homoerotic. Pragmatically, both great writers were autoerotic, though Andersen's longings for women were more poignant than Whitman's largely literary gestures towards heterosexuality. But Whitman was a poet-prophet, who offered salvation, hardly Christian. Andersen professed a rather sentimental devotion to the Christ child, but his art is pagan in nature. His Danish contemporary, Kierkegaard, shrewdly sensed this early on. From the perspective of the twenty-first century, Andersen and Kierkegaard strangely divide between them the aesthetic eminence of Danish literature. In this introduction to a volume of Andersen-criticism, I want to define precisely the qualities of Andersen's stories that go on making them imperishable, as we approach the bicentennial of his birth in 2005. Kierkegaard himself rightly analyzed his own project as the illumination of how impossible it is to become a Christian in an ostensibly Christian society. Andersen covertly had a rather different project: how to remain a child in an ostensibly adult world.

I myself see no distinction between children's literature and good or great writing for extremely intelligent children of all ages. J.K. Rowling and Stephen King are equally bad writers, appropriate titans of our new Dark Age of the Screens: computer, motion pictures, television. One goes on urging children of all ages to read and reread Andersen and Dickens, Lewis Carroll and James Joyce, rather than Rowling and King. Sometimes when I say that in public I am asked afterwards: it is not better to read Rowling and King, and then go on to Andersen, Dickens, Carroll and Joyce? The answer is pragmatic: our time here is limited. You necessarily read and reread at the expense of other books. If we lived for several centuries, there might be world enough and time, but the reality principle forces us to choose.

I have just read through the twenty-two *Stories of Hans Christian Andersen*, a new translation from the Danish by Diana Crone Frank and Jeffrey Frank. Andersen called his memoir *The Fairy Tale of My Life*, and it makes clear how painful was his emergence from the working class of Denmark in the early nineteenth century. The driving purpose of his career was to win fame and honor while not forgetting how hard the way up had been. His memories of being read to by his father from *The Arabian Nights* seem stronger than those of the actual circumstances of his upbringing. Absorbing the biographies of Andersen is a curious process: when I stand back from what I have learned I have the impression of a remarkable directness in the teenage Andersen, who marched into Copenhagen and collapsed himself upon the kindness of strangers. This peculiar directness lasted all his life: he went throughout Europe introducing himself to Heine, Victor Hugo, Lamartine, Vigny, Mendelsohn, Schumann, Dickens, the Brownings, and many others. A hunter of big names, he hungered above all to become one himself, and won through by the invention of his fairy tales.

Anderson was an outrageously prolific author in every genre: novels, travelogues, poetry, stage plays, but he mattered and always will entirely because of his unique fairy tales, which he transmuted into a creation of his own, fusing the supernatural and the common life in ways that continue to surprise me, more even than do the tales of Hoffmann, Gogol, and Kleist, setting aside the sublimely dreadful but inescapable Poe.

Sexual frustration is Anderson's pervasive though hidden obsession, embodied in his witches and icy temptresses, and in his androgynous princes. The progress of his fairy stories marches through more than forty years of visions and revisions, and even now has not been fully studied. Here I will give brief critical impressions and appreciations of six tales: "The Little Mermaid" (1837), "The Wild Swans (1838), "The Snow

Queen" (1845), "The Red Shoes" (1845), "The Shadow" (1847), and "Auntie Toothache" (1872).

On its vivid surfaces "The Little Mermaid" suggests a parable of renunciation, and yet in my own literary sense of the tale, it is a horror story, centering upon the very scary figure of the sea witch:

> She came to a large slimy clearing in the forest, where big fat water snakes gamboled and showed off their disgusting yellow-white undersides. In the middle of the clearing was a house built out of the white skeletons of shipwrecked humans; that was where the sea witch sat with a toad that she let eat out of her mouth the same way that people let a little canary eat sugar. She called the fat ugly water snakes her little chickens, and let them frolic on her huge spongy chest.
>
> "I think I know what you want," the sea witch said. "You are being very unwise. You can have it your way, but it's going to bring you grief, my lovely princess. You want to get rid of your fish tail and replace it with two stumps to walk on, like a human, so the young prince will fall in love with you, and you will have him and an immortal soul."
>
> At that, the sea witch laughed so loudly and nastily that the toad and snakes fell to the ground and rolled around. "You came just in time," the witch said. "After sunrise tomorrow I wouldn't have been able to help you for another year. I'll make you a drink, but before the sun comes up, you must swim to land, sit on the shore, and drink it. Then your tail will split in two and shrink into what humans call 'pretty legs.' But it hurts—it's like a sharp sword going through you. Everyone who sees you will say that you're the loveliest girl that they have ever seen. You will keep your gliding walk; no dancer will soar like you. But every step you take will feel like you are stepping on a sharp knife that makes you bleed. If you're willing to suffer all this, I'll help you."
>
> "Yes!" the little mermaid said in a quivering voice, and she thought about the prince and about winning an immortal soul.
>
> "But remember," the sea witch continued, as soon as you get a human form, you can't ever be a mermaid again. You can never swim down through the water to your sisters and your father's castle. And unless you win the prince's love so that he forgets his father and mother for your sake and thinks only about you and lets the pastor put your hands together so that you become man and wife, you won't get an immortal soul.

The first morning after he has married someone else, your heart will break, and you'll turn into foam on the sea."

"I still want to do it," the little mermaid said. She was pale as a corpse.

"But you have to pay me too," the Sea Witch went on, "and I ask for quite a bit. You have the prettiest voice of anyone on the bottom of the sea, and I'm sure you imagine that you'll charm him. But you have to give me that voice. I want the most precious thing you own for my precious drink. As you know, I have to add my own blood to make the drink as sharp as a double-edged sword."

"But if you take my voice," the little mermaid said, "what will I have left?"

"Your beautiful figure," the witch said, "your soaring walk, and your eloquent eyes—with all that you can certainly enchant a human heart. Well, well—have you lost heart? Stick out your little tongue. Then I'll cut it off as payment, and you'll get my powerful drink."

There is a peculiar ghastliness about this, virtually unmatched in literary fantasy. It has the aesthetic dignity of great art, yet a shudder goes with it. Andersen's imagination is as cruel as it is powerful, and "The Little Mermaid" is least persuasive (to me) in its benign conclusion. The story should end when the mermaid leaps from ship to sea and feels her body dissolve into foam. Something in Andersen could not abide in this nihilistic sacrifice, and so he allows an Ascension in which his heroine joins the daughters of the air, thus recovering her voice. The aesthetic difficulty is not sentimentality but sublimation, a defense against the erotic drive that may work for the rare saint but almost never in imaginative literature.

There is no consistent allegory in "The Little Mermaid," and whoever finds a moral in it should be shot, a remark I intend in the spirit of Mark Twain rather than the mode of Flannery O'Connor. I prefer Andersen's revision of a Danish folktale, "The Wild Swans," which culminates in utter ambivalence when another mute maiden, the beautiful Elisa, undergoes a second marriage with a king so doltish he nearly burns her alive as a witch, at the prompting of an evil archbishop. The weird remarriage is appropriate in a tale where Elisa's eleven brothers experience a radical daily metamorphosis into eleven wild swans:

"We brothers," the oldest said, "are wild swans as long as the sun is up. When it sets, we get our human shape back. That's why we always have to make sure that we have solid ground underfoot when the sun sets. If we were flying among the clouds, we would, as human beings, plunge into the deep. We can't stay here, but there's a country as beautiful as this one on the other side of the ocean. It's a long distance. We have to cross the big ocean, and there are no islands on the way where we can stay for the night—only a solitary little rock juts up in the middle of the sea. It's just big enough for us to rest on side by side, and when the sea is rough, the water sprays high above us.

That vision has the strangeness of lasting myth. There are disturbing overtones here. Are we, in our youth, wild swans by day, and human again only at night, resting on a solitary spot in the midst of an abyss? Meditating upon the self of half-a-century ago, at seventy-four I am moved to a Shakespearean sense of wonder by Andersen's marvelous extended metaphor.

In two famous stories of 1845, as he reaches meridian, Andersen achieved a fresh power of imagination. "The Snow Queen" is called by Andersen a tale in seven stories, or an "ice puzzle of the mind," a marvelous phrase taken from and alluding to the unfinished visionary novel of Novalis, *Heinrich von Ofterdingen*. Its evil troll, the Devil himself, makes a mirror, eventually fragmented, that is the essence of reductiveness; that is, what any person or thing is *really* like is simply the worst way it can be viewed. At the center of Andersen's tale are two children who at first defy all reductiveness: Gerda and Kai. They are poor, but while not sister and brother, they share fraternal love. The beautiful but icy Snow Queen abducts Kai, and Gerda goes in quest of him. An old witch, benign but possessive, appropriates Gerda, who departs for the wide world to continue her search for Kai. But my summary is a hopeless parody of Andersen's blithe irony of a narrative, where even the most menacing entities pass by in a phantasmagoric rush: talking reindeer, a bandit girl who offers friendship even as she waves a knife, the Northern Lights, living snowflakes. When Gerda finds Kai in the Snow Queen's castle, she warms him with kisses until he unthaws. Redeemed, they journey home together to a perpetual summer of happiness, ambiguously sexual.

The fascination of "The Snow Queen" is Gerda's continuous resourcefulness and strength, which derives from her freedom or refusal of all reductiveness. She is an implicit defense of Anderson's power as a story teller, his endless self-reliance. Perhaps Gerda is Andersen's answer to Kierkegaard, hardly his admirer. Gerda can be set against Kierkegaard at his uncanniest: *The Concept of Dread, The Sickness Unto Death, Fear and*

Trembling, Repetition. The titles themselves belong to the Snow Queen's realm, and not to Gerda's and Andersen's.

The alarming and famous story, "The Red Shoes," always has frightened me. The beautiful red dancing shoes whirl Karen into a cursed existence of perpetual motion, that cannot be solved even when her feet (with her consent) are cut off. Only her sanctified death accomplishes liberation. Darkly enigmatic, Andersen's tale hints at what Freud called over-determination, and renders Karen into the antithesis of Gerda.

"The Shadow," composed during a hot Naples summer of 1847, may be Andersen's most evasive masterpiece. The author and his shadow disengage from one another, in the tradition of tales by Chamisso and Hoffmann, and Andersen's shadow is malign and Iago-like. He comes back to Andersen, and persuades him to be a travel-companion, but as the shadow of his own shadow, as it were. The reader begins to suffer a metaphysical bewilderment, augmented by the involvement of a princess who sees too clearly, yet takes the original shadow as her consort. Andersen threatens exposure of identity, and is imprisoned by his former shadow, and soon enough is executed. This crazy and embittered parable prophesies Kafka, Borges, and Calvino, but more interestingly it returns us to everything problematic and ambivalent about Andersen's relation both to himself and to his art.

My ultimate favorite story by Andersen is his chillingly hilarious "Auntie Toothache," composed less than three years before his death. He may have intended it as his *logos* or defining Word, and it is spoken by Andersen himself in the first person. As an inventor of a laughter that hurts, Andersen follows Shakespeare and prophesies Philip Roth. There is no figure in Andersen more menacing than Auntie Toothache:

> A figure sat on the floor; it was thin and long, like those that a child draws with a pencil on a slate. It was supposed to look like a person: Its body was a single thin line; another two lines made the arms, the legs were single lines too, and the head was all angles.
>
> The figure soon became clearer. It wore a kind of dress— very thin, very fine—that showed that the figure belonged to the female sex.
>
> I heard a humming. Was it her or was it the wind that buzzed like a horsefly in the crack of the windowpane?
>
> No, it was Madame Toothache herself—Her Frightfulness, *Satania infernalis*, God save us from her visit.
>
> "This is a nice place to live," she hummed. "It's a good

neighborhood—swampy, boggy ground. Mosquitoes used to buzz by here with poison in their sting. Now I'm the one with the stinger. It has to be sharpened on human teeth, and that fellow on the bed has such shiny white ones. They've held their own against sweet and sour, hot and cold, nutshells and plum pits. But I'm going to wiggle them, jiggle them, feed them with a draft, and chill them at their roots."

As Her Frightfulness says: "Great poets must have great toothaches; small poets, small toothaches." There is a vertigo in the story: we cannot know whether Auntie Toothache and the amiable Aunt Millie (who encourages Andersen's poetry) are one person or two. The penultimate sentence is: "Everything goes into the trash."

The accent is of Koheleth (Ecclesiastes): all is vanity. Andersen was a visionary tale-teller, but his fairy-realm was malign. Of his aesthetic eminence, I entertain no doubts, but I believe that we still have not learned how to read him.

Edgar Allan Poe

(1809–1849)

CRITICS, EVEN GOOD ONES, ADMIRE POE'S STORIES FOR SOME OF THE ODDEST of reasons. Poe, a true Southerner, abominated Emerson, plainly perceiving that Emerson (like Whitman, like Lincoln) was not a Christian, not a royalist, not a classicist. Self-reliance, the Emersonian answer to Original Sin, does not exist in the Poe cosmos, where you necessarily start out damned, doomed, and dismal. But I think Poe detested Emerson for some of the same reasons Hawthorne and Melville more subtly resented him, reasons that persist in the most distinguished living American writer, Robert Penn Warren, and in many current academic literary critics in our country. If you dislike Emerson, you probably will like Poe. Emerson fathered pragmatism; Poe fathered precisely nothing, which is the way he would have wanted it. Yvor Winters accused Poe of obscurantism, but that truthful indictment no more damages Poe than does tastelessness and tone deafness. Emerson, for better and for worse, was and is the mind of America, but Poe was and is our hysteria, our uncanny unanimity in our repressions. I certainly do not intend to mean by this that Poe was deeper than Emerson in any way whatsoever. Emerson cheerfully and consciously threw out the past. Critics tend to share Poe's easy historicism; perhaps without knowing it, they are gratified that every Poe story is, in too clear a sense, over even as it begins. We don't have to wait for Madeline Usher and the house to fall in upon poor Roderick; they have fallen in upon him already, before the narrator comes upon the place. Emerson exalted freedom, which he and Thoreau usefully called "wildness." No one in Poe is or can be free or wild, and some academic admirers of Poe truly like everything and everyone to be in bondage to a universal past. To begin is to be free, godlike and Emersonian-Adamic, or Jeffersonian. But for a writer to be free is bewildering and even maddening. What American writers and their exegetes half-unknowingly love in Poe is his more-than-Freudian oppressive and curiously original sense and sensation of overdetermination. Walter Pater once remarked that museums depressed him because they made him doubt that anyone ever had once been young. No one in a Poe story ever was young. As D.H. Lawrence angrily observed, everyone in Poe is a vampire—Poe himself in particular.

II

Among Poe's tales, the near-exception to what I have been saying is the longest and most ambitious, *The Narrative of Arthur Gordon Pym*, just as the best of Poe's poems is the long prose-poem *Eureka*. Alas, even these works are somewhat overvalued, if only because Poe's critics understandably become excessively eager to see him vindicated. *Pym* is readable, but *Eureka* is extravagantly repetitious. Auden was quite taken with *Eureka*, but could remember very little of it in conversation, and one can doubt that he read it through, at least in English. Poe's most advanced critic is John T. Irwin, in his book *American Hieroglyphics*. Irwin rightly centers upon *Pym*, while defending *Eureka* as an "aesthetic cosmology" addressed to what in each of us Freud called the "bodily ego." Irwin is too shrewd to assert that Poe's performance in *Eureka* fulfills Poe's extraordinary intentions:

> What the poem *Eureka*, at once pre-Socratic and post-Newtonian, asserts is the truth of the feeling, the bodily intuition, that the diverse objects which the mind discovers in contemplating external nature form a unity, that they are all parts of one body which, if not infinite, is so gigantic as to be beyond both the spatial and temporal limits of human perception. In *Eureka*, then, Poe presents us with the paradox of a "unified" macrocosmic body that is without a totalizing image—an alogical, intuitive belief whose "truth" rests upon Poe's sense that cosmologies and myths of origin are forms of internal geography that, under the guise of mapping the physical universe, map the universe of desire.

Irwin might be writing of Blake, or of other visionaries who have sought to map total forms of desire. What Irwin catches, by implication, is Poe's troubling anticipation of what is most difficult in Freud, the "frontier concepts" between mind and body, such as the bodily ego, the non-repressive defense of introjection, and above all, the drives or instincts.

Poe, not just in *Eureka* and in *Pym*, but throughout his tales and even in some of his verse, is peculiarly close to the Freudian speculation upon the bodily ego. Freud, in *The Ego and the Id* (1923), resorted to the uncanny language of E.T.A. Hoffmann (and of Poe) in describing this difficult notion:

> The ego is first and foremost a bodily ego; it is not merely a surface entity, but is itself the projection of a surface. If we wish to find an anatomical analogy for it we can best identify it with the "cortical homunculus" of the anatomists, which stands on its head in the cortex, sticks up its heels, faces backwards and, as we know, has its speech-area on the left-hand side.

A footnote in the English translation of 1927, authorized by Freud but never added to the German editions, elucidates the first sentence of this description in a way analogous to the crucial metaphor in Poe that concludes *The Narrative of Arthur Gordon Pym*:

> I.e. the ego is ultimately derived from bodily sensations, chiefly from those springing from the surface of the body, besides, as we have seen above, representing the superficies of the mental apparatus.

A considerable part of Poe's mythological power emanates from his own difficult sense that the ego is always a bodily ego. The characters of Poe's tales live out nearly every conceivable fantasy of introjection and identification, seeking to assuage their melancholia by psychically devouring the lost objects of their affections. D.H. Lawrence, in his *Studies in Classic American Literature* (1923), moralized powerfully against Poe, condemning him for "the will-to-love and the will-to-consciousness, asserted against death itself. The pride of human conceit in KNOWLEDGE." It is illuminating that Lawrence attacked Poe in much the same spirit as he attacked Freud, who is interpreted in *Psychoanalysis and the Unconscious* as somehow urging us to violate the taboo against incest. The interpretation is as extravagant as Lawrence's thesis that Poe urged vampirism upon us, but there remains something suggestive in Lawrence's violence against both Freud and Poe. Each placed the elitist individual in jeopardy, Lawrence implied, by hinting at the primacy of fantasy not just in the sexual life proper, but in the bodily ego's constitution of itself through acts of incorporation and identification.

The cosmology of *Eureka* and the narrative of *Pym* alike circle around fantasies of incorporation. *Eureka's* subtitle is "An Essay on the Material and Spiritual Universe" and what Poe calls its "general proposition" is heightened by italics: "*In the Original Unity of the First Thing lies the Secondary Cause of all Things, with the Germ of their Inevitable Annihilation.*" Freud, in his cosmology, Beyond the Pleasure Principle, posited that the inorganic had preceded the organic, and also that it was the tendency of all things to return to their original state. Consequently, the aim of all life was death. The death drive, which became crucial for Freud's later dualisms, is nevertheless pure mythology, since Freud's only evidence for it was the repetition compulsion, and it is an extravagant leap from repetition to death. This reliance upon one's own mythology may have prompted Freud's audacity when, in the *New Introductory Lectures*, he admitted that the theory of drives was, so to speak, his own mythology, drives being not only magnificent conceptions but particularly sublime in their indefiniteness. I wish I could assert that *Eureka* has some of the speculative force of *Beyond the Pleasure Principle* or even of Freud's disciple Ferenczi's startling *Thalassa: A Theory of Genitality*; but *Eureka* does badly enough when compared to Emerson's *Nature*, which itself has only a few passages worthy of what Emerson wrote afterwards. And yet Valéry in one sense was justified in his praise for *Eureka*. For certain intellectuals, *Eureka* performs a mythological function akin to what Poe's tales continue to do for hosts of readers. *Eureka* is unevenly written, badly repetitious, and sometimes opaque in its abstractness, but like the tales it seems not to have been composed by a particular individual. The universalism of a common nightmare informs it. If the tales lose little, or even gain, when we retell them to others in our own words, *Eureka* gains by Valéry's observations, or by the summaries of recent critics like John Irwin or Daniel Hoffman. Translation even into his own language always benefits Poe.

I haven't the space, or the desire, to summarize *Eureka*, and no summary is likely to do anything besides deadening both my readers and myself. Certainly Poe was never more passionately sincere than in composing *Eureka*, of which he affirmed: "*What I here propound is true.*" But these are the closing sentences of *Eureka*:

> Think that the sense of individual identity will be gradually merged in the general consciousness—that Man, for example, ceasing imperceptibly to feel himself Man, will at length attain that awfully triumphant epoch when he shall recognize his existence as that of Jehovah. In the meantime bear in mind that all is Life—Life—Life within Life—the less within the greater, and all within the *Spirit Divine*.

To this, Poe appends a "Note":

> The pain of the consideration that we shall lose our individual
> identity, ceases at once when we further reflect that the process,
> as above described, is, neither more nor less than that of the
> absorption, by each individual intelligence of all other intelli-
> gences (that is, of the Universe) into its own. That God may be
> all in all, *each* must become God.

Allen Tate, not unsympathetic to his cousin, Mr. Poe, remarked of
Poe's extinction in *Eureka* that "there is a lurid sublimity in the spectacle
of his taking God along with him into a grave which is not smaller than the
universe." If we read closely, Poe's trope is "absorption," and we are where
we always are in Poe, amid ultimate fantasies of introjection in which the
bodily ego and the cosmos become indistinguishable. Again, I suspect this
judgment hardly weakens Poe, since his strength is no more cognitive than
it is stylistic. Poe's mythology, like the mythology of psychoanalysis that we
cannot yet bear to acknowledge as primarily a mythology, is peculiarly
appropriate to any modernism, whether you want to call it early, high or
post-modernism. The definitive judgment belongs here to T.W. Adorno,
certainly the most authentic theoretician of all modernisms, in his last
book, *Aesthetic Theory*. Writing on "reconciliation and mimetic adaptation
to death," Adorno blends the insights of Jewish negative theology and psychoanalysis:

> Whether negativity is the barrier or the truth of art is not for
> art to decide. Art works are negative *per se* because they are sub-
> ject to the law of objectification; that is, they kill what they
> objectify, tearing it away from its context of immediacy and real
> life. They survive because they bring death. This is particular-
> ly true of modern art, where we notice a general mimetic aban-
> donment to reification, which is the principle of death. Illusion
> in art is the attempt to escape from this principle. Baudelaire
> marks a watershed, in that art after him seeks to discard illusion
> without resigning itself to being a thing among things. The
> harbingers of modernism, Poe and Baudelaire, were the first
> technocrats of art.

Baudelaire was more than a technocrat of art, as Adorno knew, but
Poe would be only that except for his mythmaking gift. C.S. Lewis may
have been right when he insisted that such a gift could exist even apart

from other literary endowments. Blake and Freud are inescapable myth-makers who were also cognitively and stylistically powerful. Poe is a great fantasist whose thoughts were commonplace and whose metaphors were dead. Fantasy, mythologically considered, combines the stances of Narcissus and Prometheus, which are ideologically antithetical to one another, but figuratively quite compatible. Poe is at once the Narcissus and the Prometheus of his nation. If that is right, then he is inescapable, even though his tales contrast weakly with Hawthorne's, his poems scarcely bear reading, and his speculative discourses fade away in juxtaposition to Emerson's, his despised Northern rival.

III

To define Poe's mythopoeic inevitability more closely, I turn to his story "Ligeia" and to the end of *Pym*. Ligeia, a tall, dark, slender transcendentalist, dies murmuring a protest against the feeble human will, which cannot keep us forever alive. Her distraught and nameless widower, the narrator, endeavors to comfort himself, first with opium, and then with a second bride, "the fair-haired and blue-eyed Lady Rowena Trevanian, of Tremaine." Unfortunately, he has little use for this replacement, and so she sickens rapidly and dies. Recurrently, the corpse revivifies, only to die yet again and again. At last, the cerements are stripped away, and the narrator confronts the undead Ligeia, attired in the death-draperies of her now evaporated successor.

As a parable of the vampiric will, this works well enough. The learned Ligeia presumably has completed her training in the will during her absence, or perhaps merely owes death a substitute, the insufficiently transcendental Rowena. What is mythopoeically more impressive is the ambiguous question of the narrator's will. Poe's own life, like Walt Whitman's, is an American mythology, and what all of us generally remember about it is that Poe married his first cousin, Virginia Clemm, before she turned fourteen. She died a little more than ten years later, having been a semi-invalid for most of that time. Poe himself died less than three years after her, when he was just forty. "Ligeia," regarded by Poe as his best tale, was written a bit more than a year into the marriage. The later Freud implicitly speculates that there are no accidents; we die because we will to die, our character being also our fate. In Poe's myth also, ethos is the daemon, and the daemon is our destiny. The year after Virginia died, Poe proposed marriage to the widowed poet Sarah Helen Whitman. Biographers tell us that the lady's doubts were caused by rumors of Poe's bad character, but perhaps Mrs. Whitman had read "Ligeia"! In any event, this marriage did not take place, nor did Poe survive to marry another widow, his childhood sweetheart Elmira Royster Shelton. Perhaps she too might have read "Ligeia" and forborne.

The narrator of "Ligeia" has a singularly bad memory, or else a very curious relationship to his own will, since he begins by telling us that he married Ligeia without ever having troubled to learn her family name. Her name itself is legend, or romance, and that was enough. As the story's second paragraph hints, the lady was an opium dream with the footfall of a shadow. The implication may be that there never was such a lady, or even that if you wish to incarnate your reveries, then you must immolate your consubstantial Rowena. What is a touch alarming to the narrator is the intensity of Ligeia's passion for him, which was manifested however only by glances and voice so long as the ideal lady lived. Perhaps this baffled intensity is what kills Ligeia, through a kind of narcissistic dialectic, since she is dominated not by the will of her lust but by the lust of her will. She wills her infinite passion towards the necessarily inadequate narrator and when (by implication) he fails her, she turns the passion of her will against dying and at last against death. Her dreadful poem, "The Conqueror Worm," prophesies her cyclic return from death: "Through a circle that ever returneth in / To the self-same spot." But when she does return, the spot is hardly the same. Poor Rowena only becomes even slightly interesting to her narrator-husband when she sickens unto death, and her body is wholly usurped by the revived Ligeia. And yet the wretched narrator is a touch different, if only because his narcissism is finally out of balance with his first wife's grisly Prometheanism. There are no final declarations of Ligeia's passion as the story concludes. The triumph of her will is complete, but we know that the narrator's will has not blent itself into Ligeia's. His renewed obsession with her eyes testifies to a continued sense of her daemonic power over him, but his final words hint at what the story's opening confirms: she will not be back for long—and remains "my lost love."

The conclusion of Pym has been brilliantly analyzed by John Irwin, and so I want to glance only briefly at what is certainly Poe's most effective closure:

> And now we rushed into the embraces of the cataract, where a chasm threw itself open to receive us. But there arose in our pathway a shrouded human figure, very far larger in its proportions than any dweller among men. And the hue of the skin of the figure was of the perfect whiteness of the snow.

Irwin demonstrates Poe's reliance here upon the Romantic topos of the Alpine White Shadow, the magnified projection of the observer himself. The chasm Pym enters is the familiar Romantic Abyss, not a part of the natural world but belonging to eternity, before the creation. Reflected in that abyss, Pym beholds his own shrouded form, perfect in the whiteness of the natural context. Presumably, this is the original bodily ego, the Gnostic self before the fall into creation. As at the close of *Eureka*, Poe brings Alpha and Omega together in an apocalyptic circle. I suggest we read Pym's, which is to say Poe's, white shadow as the American triumph of the will, as illusory as Ligeia's usurpation of Rowena's corpse.

Poe teaches us, through Pym and Ligeia, that as Americans we are both subject and object to our own quests. Emerson, in Americanizing the European sense of the abyss, kept the self and the abyss separate as facts: "There may be two or three or four steps, according to the genius of each, but for every seeing soul there are two absorbing facts—I and the Abyss." Poe, seeking to avoid Emersonianism, ends with only one fact, and it is more a wish than a fact: "I will to be the Abyss." This metaphysical despair has appealed to the Southern American literary tradition and to its Northern followers. The appeal cannot be refuted, because it is myth, and Poe backed the myth with his life as well as his work. If the Northern or Emersonian myth of our literary culture culminates in the beautiful image of Walt Whitman as wound-dresser, moving as a mothering father through the Civil War Washington, D.C., hospitals, then the Southern or countermyth achieves its perfect stasis at its start, with Poe's snow-white shadow shrouding the chasm down which the boat of the soul is about to plunge. Poe's genius was for negativity and opposition, and the affirmative force of Emersonian America gave him the impetus his daemonic will required.

IV

It would be a relief to say that Poe's achievement as a critic is not mythological, but the splendid, new and almost complete edition of his essays, reviews and marginalia testifies otherwise. It shows Poe indeed to have been Adorno's "technocrat of art." Auden defended Poe's criticism by contrasting the subjects Baudelaire was granted—Delacroix, Constantin Guys, Wagner—with the books Poe was given to review, such as *The Christian Florist*, *The History of Texas*, and *Poetical Remains of the Late Lucretia Maria Davidson*. The answer to Auden is that Poe also wrote about Bryant, Byron, Coleridge, Dickens, Hawthorne, Washington Irving, Longfellow, Shelley, and Tennyson; a ninefold providing scope enough for any authentic critical consciousness. Nothing that Poe had to say about these poets and storytellers is in any way memorable or at all an aid to reading them. There are no critical insights, no original perceptions, no accurate or illuminating juxtapositions or historical placements. Here is Poe on Tennyson, from his *Marginalia*, which generally surpasses his other criticism:

> Why do some persons fatigue themselves in attempts to unravel such phantasy-pieces as the "Lady of Shalott"? ... If the author did not deliberately propose to himself a suggestive indefinitiveness of meaning, with the view of bringing about a definitiveness of vague and therefore of spiritual *effect*—this, at least, arose from the silent analytical promptings of that poetic genius which, in its supreme development, embodies all orders of intellectual capacity.

I take this as being representative of Poe's criticism, because it is uninterestingly just plain *wrong* about "The Lady of Shalott." No other poem, even by the great word-painter Tennyson, is deliberately so definite in meaning and effect. Everything vague precisely is excluded in this perhaps most Pre-Raphaelite of all poems, where each detail contributes to an impression that might be called hard-edged phantasmagoria. If we take as the three possibilities of nineteenth-century practical criticism the sequence of Arnold, Pater, and Wilde, we find Poe useless in all three modes: Arnold's seeing the object as in itself it really is, Pater's seeing accurately one's own impression of the object, and the divine Oscar's sublime seeing of the object as in itself it really is not. If "The Lady of Shalott" is the object, then Poe does not see anything: the poem as in itself it is, one's impression of the poem as that is, or best of all the Wildean sense of what is missing or excluded from the poem. Poe's descriptive terms are "indefinitiveness" and "vague," but Tennyson's poem is just the reverse:

> She left the web, she left the loom,
> She made three paces through the room,
> She saw the water-lily bloom,
> She saw the helmet and the plume,
>   She looked down to Camelot.
> Out flew the web and floated wide;
> The mirror cracked from side to side;
> "The curse is come upon me," cried
>   The Lady of Shalott.

No, Poe as practical critic is a true match for most of his contemporary subjects, such as S. Anna Lewis, author of *The Child of the Sea and Other Poems* (1848). Of her lyric "The Forsaken," Poe wrote, "We have read this little poem more than twenty times and always with increasing admiration. *It is inexpressibly beautiful*" (Poe's italics). I quote only the first of its six stanzas:

> It hath been said—for all who die
>   there is a tear;
> Some pining, bleeding heart to sigh
>   O'er every bier:
> But in that hour of pain and dread
>   Who will draw near
> Around my humble couch and shed
>   One farewell tear?

Well, but there is Poe as theoretician, Valéry has told us. Acute self-consciousness in Poe was strongly misread by Valéry as the inauguration and development of severe and skeptical ideas. Presumably, this is the Poe of three famous essays: "The Philosophy of Composition," "The Rationale of Verse," and "The Poetic Principle." Having just reread these pieces, I have no possibility of understanding a letter of Valéry to Mallarmé which prizes the theories of Poe as being "so profound and so insidiously learned." Certainly we prize the theories of Valéry for just those qualities, and so I have come full circle to where I began, with the mystery of French Poe. Valéry may be said to have read Poe in the critical modes both of Pater and of Wilde. He saw his impression of Poe clearly, and he saw Poe's essays as in themselves they really were not. Admirable, and so Valéry brought to culmination the critical myth that is French Poe.

V

> Whose head is swinging from the swollen strap?
> Whose body smokes along the bitten rails,
> Bursts from a smoldering bundle far behind
> In back forks of the chasms of the brain—
> Puffs from a riven stump far out behind
> In interborough fissures of the mind ...?

Hart Crane's vision of Poe, in the "Tunnel" section of *The Bridge*, tells us again why the mythopoeic Poe is inescapable for American literary mythology. Poe's nightmare projections and introjections suggest the New York City subway as the new underground, where Coleridge's "deep Romantic chasm" has been internalized into "the chasms of the brain." Whatever his actual failures as poet and critic, whatever the gap between style and idea in his tales, Poe is central to the American canon, both for us and for the rest of the world. Hawthorne implicitly and Melville explicitly made far more powerful critiques of the Emersonian national hope, but they were by no means wholly negative in regard to Emerson and his pragmatic vision of American Self-Reliance. Poe was savage in denouncing minor transcendentalists like Bronson Alcott and William Ellery Channing, but his explicit rejection of Emerson confined itself to the untruthful observation that Emerson was indistinguishable from Thomas Carlyle. Poe should have survived to read Carlyle's insane and amazing pamphlet "The Nigger Question," which he would have adored. Mythologically, Poe is necessary because all of his work is a hymn to negativity. Emerson was a great theoretician of literature as of life, a good practical critic (when he wanted to be, which was not often), a very good poet (sometimes) and always a major aphorist and essayist. Poe, on a line-by-line or sentence-by-sentence basis, is hardly a worthy opponent. But looking in the French way, as T.S. Eliot recommended, "we see a mass of unique shape and impressive size to which the eye constantly returns." Eliot was probably right, in mythopoeic terms.

Nikolai Gogol

(1809–1852)

DOSTOEVSKY FAMOUSLY SAID: "WE ALL CAME OUT FROM UNDER GOGOL'S 'Overcoat,'" a short story concerning a wretched copying clerk whose new overcoat is stolen. Disdained by the authorities, to whom he duly protests, the poor fellow dies, after which his ghost continues to search vainly for justice. Good as the story is, it is not the best of Gogol, which may be "Old-World Landowners" or the insane "The Nose," which begins when a barber, at breakfast, discovers a customer's nose inside a loaf of bread freshly baked by his wife. The spirit of Gogol, subtly alive in much of Nabokov, achieves its apotheosis in the triumphant "Gogol's Wife," by the modern Italian story-writer Tommaso Landolfi, perhaps the funniest and most unnerving story that I've yet read.

The narrator, Gogol's friend and biographer, "reluctantly" tells us the story of Gogol's wife. The actual Gogol, a religious obsessive, never married, and deliberately starved himself to death at forty-three or so, after burning his unpublished manuscripts. But Landolfi's Gogol (who might have been invented by Kafka or by Borges) has married a rubber balloon, a splendidly inflatable dummy who assumes different shapes and sizes at her husband's whim. Much in love with his wife, in one of her forms or another, Gogol enjoys sexual relations with her, and bestows upon her the name Caracas, after the capital of Venezuela, for reasons known only to the mad writer.

For some years, all goes well, until Gogol contracts syphilis, which he rather unfairly blames upon Caracas. Ambivalence towards his silent wife gains steadily in Gogol through the years. He accuses Caracas of self-gratification, and even betrayal, so that she becomes bitter and excessively religious. Finally, the enraged Gogol pumps too much air into Caracas (quite deliberately) until she bursts and scatters into the air. Collecting the remnants of Madame Gogol, the great writer burns them in the fireplace, where they share the fate of his unpublished works. Into the same fire, Gogol casts also a rubber doll, the son of Caracas. After this final catastrophe, the biographer defends Gogol from the charge of wife-beating, and salutes the memory of the writer's lofty genius.

The best prelude (or postlude) to reading Landolfi's "Gogol's Wife" is to read some stories by Gogol, on the basis of which we will not doubt the reality of the unfortunate Caracas. She is as likely a paramour as Gogol could ever have discovered (or invented) for himself. In contrast, Landolfi could hardly have composed much the same story and called it "Maupassant's Wife," let alone "Turgenev's Wife." No, it has to be Gogol and Gogol alone, and I rarely doubt Landolfi's story, particularly just after each rereading. Caracas has a reality that Borges neither seeks nor achieves for his Tlön. As Gogol's only possible bride, she seems to me the ultimate parody of Frank O'Connor's insistence that the lonely voice crying out in the modern short story is that of the Submerged Population. Who could be more submerged than Gogol's wife?

Ivan Turgenev

(1818-1883)

MY FAVORITES AMONG THE *SPORTSMAN'S SKETCHES* ARE "BEZHIN LEA" AND "Kasyan from the Beautiful Lands," but as I have written about them in *How to Read and Why* (2000), I turn here to "Forest and Steppe," the last of the *Sketches*.

With Chekhov, Turgenev invented one prevalent mode of the modern short story, challenged later by the irreality of what could be called the Kafka-Borges tradition. The aesthetic splendor of Turgenev's *Sketches* partly depends upon the writer's apprehension of natural beauty: this hunter's quarry is not so much game as vista.

"Forest and Steppe" begins by emphasizing the hunter's solitary joy:

> By the time you've travelled two miles or so the rim of the sky is beginning to crimson; in the birches jackdaws are awakening and clumsily fluttering from branch to branch; sparrows twitter about the dark hayricks. The air grows brighter, the road clearer, the sky lightens, suffusing the clouds with whiteness and the fields with green. Lights burn red in the cottages and sleepy voices can be heard beyond the gates. In the meantime dawn has burst into flame; stripes of gold have risen across the sky and wreaths of mist form in the ravines; to the loud singing of skylarks and the soughing of the wind before dawn the sun rises, silent and purple, above the horizon. Light floods over the world and your heart trembles within you like a bird. Everything is so fresh, gay and lovely! You can see for miles. Here a village glimmers beyond the woodland; there, farther away, is another village with a white church and then a hill with a birchwood; beyond it is the marsh to which you are driving ...

Step lively there, horses! Forward at a brisk trot! ... No more than two miles to go now. The sun is rising quickly, the sky is clear ... The weather will be perfect. You meet a herd of cattle coming in a long line from the village. Then you ascend the hill ... What a view! The river winds away for seven miles or more, a faint blue glimmer through the mist; beyond it are the water-green meadows: beyond them, low-lying hills; in the distance lapwings veer and cry above the marsh; through the gleaming moisture which pervades the air the distance emerges clearly ... there is no summer haze. How freely one breathes the air into one's lungs, how buoyant are one's limbs, how strong one feels in the grip of this fresh springtime atmosphere!

The line of descent to Hemingway's Nick Adams stories is clear: the issue is solitary freedom, Hemingway's "living your life all the way up." You and your dog are at last alone together in the forest, and you behold a totality of vision:

You walk along the edge of the forest, keeping your eyes on the dog, but in the meantime there come to mind beloved images, beloved faces, the living and the dead, and long-since dormant impressions unexpectedly awaken; the imagination soars and dwells on the air like a bird, and everything springs into move-ment with such clarity and stands before the eyes. Your heart either suddenly quivers and starts beating fast, passionately rac-ing forward, or drowns irretrievably in recollections. The whole of life unrolls easily and swiftly like a scroll; a man has possession of his whole past, all his feelings, all his powers, his entire soul. And nothing in his surroundings can disturb him— there is no sun, no wind, no noise ...

This vision, however individually total, knows its own limits. Yours is the freedom of the forest, and not the dismaying sublime of the steppe:

Farther, farther! The steppelands are approaching. You look down from a hill—what a view! Round, low hillocks, ploughed waves; ravines overgrown with bushes weave among them; small woods are scattered here and there like elongated islands; from village to village run narrow tracks; churches gleam white; between thickets of willow glitters a small river, its flow staunched in four places by dams; far off in the field wild cranes stick out as they waddle in file; an antiquated landowner's mansion with its outbuildings, orchard and threshing floor is settled comfortably beside a small pond. But you go on travelling, farther and farther. The hillocks grow shallower and shallower and there is hardly a tree to be seen. Finally, there it is—the limitless, enormous steppe no eye can encompass!

The *Sketches* confine themselves deliberately to what the eye can encompass. For confronting the steppe, you need to be Tolstoy, yourself a sublime nature, as strong as what you might behold. With remarkable, nuanced control, Turgenev subtly implies his own limits, and shows us again why his *Sketches* are so modulated a masterpiece.

Herman Melville

(1819–1891)

SHAKESPEARE, FOREMOST OF WRITERS, DEEPLY AFFECTED MELVILLE'S ART, both in *Moby-Dick* and in the shorter fiction. Captain Ahab broods aloud in the mode of Macbeth, while Claggart is manifestly a version of Iago. Even "Bartleby, the Scrivener," which on its surface owes more to Charles Dickens, is indebted to Shakespeare's mastery of ellipsis, the art of leaving-out. What matters most in Melville's story is never said; an enormous pathos is hinted, but is not expressed. Bartleby and the narrator barely can speak to one another, yet abysses could be explored between them. When the narrator murmurs that the dead Bartleby is asleep "With kings and counselors," we are startled by the aesthetic dignity of the Jobean but thoroughly Shakespearean evocation, and yet the surprise vanishes upon reflection. Julius Caesar and Brutus, in what should be their one crucial exchange before the scene of the assassination, share a banal moment of asking and telling the time of day. Edmund and King Lear never address one another., and except for one moment in the wings, Antony and Oeopatra are never left alone together. In the painful scene where the newly crowned Henry V rejects Falstaff, the emancipated monarch does not allow the great wit to say anything. This elliptical mode, a far more prevalent Shakespearean technique than is generally realized, prompts Melville's reticences in "Bartleby, the Scrivener."

"The Encantadas" is overtly Spenserian and Bunyanesque, but more darkly it refracts *The Tempest*. In "Sketch Seventh" the Creole Dog-King is a savage parody of Prospero, ruling his Enchanted Isle not with Ariel and a band of sprites, but with fierce dogs. "Sketch Ninth" extends the parody, when the dreadful Oberlus overtly identifies himself with Caliban: "This island's mine by Sycorax my mother." Yet Oberlus is more Timon of Athens than Caliban, and "The Encantadas" serves for Melville the purpose effected for Shakespeare by Timon of Athens, the most rancid of tragedies.

"Benito Cereno" which seems to me the masterpiece of Melville's shorter fiction, is a wonderfully enigmatic story in which Captain Delano and Benito Cereno talk past one another in ways that transcend their difficult situation, in which Delano cannot know that Cereno and his ship are the captives of a slave rebellion. Even when the rescue has been accomplished, the American and the Spanish captains are in different worlds:

> "But these mild trades that now fan your cheek. Do they not come with a human-like healing to you? Warm friends, steadfast friends are trades."
> "With their steadfastness they but waft me to my tomb, senor," was the foreboding response.
> "You are saved," cried Captain Delano, more and more astonished and pained; "you are saved; what has cast such a shadow upon you?"
> "The negro."

Prospero tells us that when he is back in Milan, every third thought shall be his grave, even though the great Magus could not be more triumphant. It is not Caliban who is Prospero's shadow of mortality, but the lost vocation of having been an Hermetic sage. Benito Cereno has more than the shadow of Babo upon him; his own vocation as sea-captain is lost, under the shadow that symbolically he terms "the negro." The inwardness of Cereno's reflection, in contrast to Delano's robust outwardness, is a Shakespearean contrast. Cereno is now lost in the growing inward self, most Shakespearean of inventions.

The Adamic Billy Budd is not a Shakespearean figure, which enhances his helplessness at confronting Iago in Claggart. The "monomania" of Claggart clearly derives from Iago's drive to ruin Othello. "Motiveless malignity," Coleridge's phrase for Iago, is far more applicable to Claggart. It would be difficult to accept Claggart, were it not for our experience of Iago. The effect of Shakespeare's Iago upon Melville's Claggart is more than a matter of influence; "contamination" would be an apter word than "influence." Claggart's "natural depravity" is an uncanny transmission from Iago to Melville's evil genius.

II

Melville's *The Piazza Tales* was published in 1856, five years after *Moby-Dick*. Two of the six tales—"Bartleby the Scrivener" and "Benito Cereno"—are commonly and rightly accepted among Melville's strongest works, together with *Moby-Dick* and (rather more tenuously) *The Confidence-Man* and *Billy Budd, Sailor*. Two others—"The Encantadas, or Enchanted Isles" and "The Bell-Tower"—seem to me even better, being equal to the best moments in *Moby-Dick*. Two of the *Piazza Tales* are relative trifles: "The Piazza" and "The Lightning-Rod Man." A volume of novellas with four near-masterpieces is an extraordinary achievement, but particularly poignant if, like Melville, you had lost your reading public after the early success of *Typee* and *Omoo*, the more equivocal reception of *Mardi*, and the return to a wider audience with *Redburn* and even more with *White Jacket*. *Moby-Dick* today is, together with *Leaves of Grass* and *Huckleberry Finn*, one of the three candidates for our national epic, but like *Leaves of Grass* it found at first only the one great reader (Hawthorne for Melville, Emerson for Whitman) and almost no popular response. What was left of Melville's early audience was killed off by the dreadful *Pierre*, a year after *Moby-Dick*, and despite various modern salvage attempts *Pierre* certainly is unreadable, in the old-fashioned sense of that now critically abused word. You just cannot get through it, unless you badly want and need to do so.

The best of *The Piazza Tales* show the post-Pierre Melville writing for himself, possibly Hawthorne, and a few strangers. Himself the sole support of wife, four children, mother, and several sisters, Melville was generally in debt from at least 1855 on, and Hawthorne and Richard Henry Dana, though they tried, could not get the author of Pierre appointed to a consulate. In the late 1850s, the tormented and shy Melville attempted the lecture circuit, but as he was neither a pulpit-pounder like Henry Ward Beecher, nor a preternaturally eloquent sage like Ralph Waldo Emerson, he failed rather badly. Unhappily married, mother-ridden, an apparent literary failure; the author of *The Piazza Tales* writes out of the depths. Steeped, as were Carlyle and Ruskin, in the King James Bible, Melville no more believed in the Bible than did Carlyle and Ruskin. But even as *Moby-Dick* found its legitimate and overwhelming precursors in the Bible, Spenser, Shakespeare, and Milton, so do *The Piazza Tales*. Melville's rejection of biblical theology, his almost Gnostic distrust of nature and history alike, finds powerful expression in *The Piazza Tales*, as it did throughout all his later fictional prose and his verse.

III

"The Bell-Tower" is a tale of only fifteen pages but it has such resonance and strength that each rereading gives me the sense that I have experienced a superb short novel. Bannadonna, "the great mechanician, the unblest foundling," seeking to conquer a larger liberty, like Prometheus, instead extended the empire of necessity. His great Bell-Tower, intended to be the noblest in Italy, survives only as "a stone pine," a "black massed stump." It is the new tower of Babel:

> Like Babel's, its base was laid in a high hour of renovated earth, following the second deluge, when the waters of the Dark Ages had dried up, and once more the green appeared. No wonder that, after so long and deep submersion, the jubilant expectation of the race should, as with Noah's sons, soar into Shinar aspiration.
>
> In firm resolve, no man in Europe at that period went beyond Bannadonna. Enriched through commerce with the Levant, the state in which he lived voted to have the noblest Bell-Tower in Italy. His repute assigned him to be architect.
>
> Stone by stone, month by month, the tower rose. Higher, higher; snail-like in pace, but torch or rocket in its pride.
>
> After the masons would depart, the builder, standing alone upon its ever-ascending summit, at close of every day, saw that he overtopped still higher walls and trees. He would tarry till a late hour there, wrapped in schemes of other and still loftier piles. Those who of saints' days thronged the spot—hanging to the rude poles of scaffolding, like sailors on yards, or bees on boughs, unmindful of lime and dust, and falling chips of stone—their homage not the less inspirited him to self-esteem.
>
> At length the holiday of the Tower came. To the sound of viols, the climax-stone slowly rose in air, and, amid the firing of ordnance, was laid by Bannadonna's hands upon the final course. Then mounting it, he stood erect, alone, with folded arms, gazing upon the white summits of blue inland Alps, and whiter crests of bluer Alps off-shore—sights invisible from the plain. Invisible, too, from thence was that eye he turned below, when, like the cannon booms, came up to him the people's combustions of applause.
>
> That which stirred them so was, seeing with what serenity the builder stood three hundred feet in air, upon an unrailed perch. This none but he durst do. But his periodic standing upon the pile, in each stage of its growth—such discipline had its last result.

We recognize Captain Ahab in Bannadonna, though Ahab has his humanities, and the great mechanician lacks all pathos. Ahab plays out an avenger's tragedy, but Bannadonna's purpose lacks any motivation except pride. His pride presumably is related to the novelist's, and the black stump that is the sole remnant of the Bell-Tower might as well be Pierre, little as Melville would have welcomed such an identification. The sexual mortification of the image is palpable, yet adds little to the comprehensiveness of what will become Bannadonna's doom, since that necessarily is enacted as a ritual of castration anyway. Melville's Prometheans, Ahab and Bannadonna, have an overtly Gnostic quarrel with the heavens. Melville's narratives, at their strongest, know implicitly what Kafka asserted with rare explicitness in his great parable:

> The crows maintain that a single crow could destroy the heavens. Doubtless that is so, but it proves nothing against the heavens for the heavens signify simply: the impossibility of crows.

In Melville, the heavens signify simply: the impossibility of Ahab and of Bannadonna. Ahab is a hunter and not a builder, but to destroy Moby-Dick or to build the Bell-Tower would be to pile up the Tower of Babel and get away with it:

> If it had been possible to build the Tower of Babel without ascending it, the work would have been permitted.

Kafka's aphorism would be an apt title for Melville's story, with Bannadonna who has built his tower partly in order to ascend it and to stand "three hundred feet in air, upon an unrailed perch." Kafka could have told Bannadonna that a labyrinth underground would have been better, though of course that too would not have been permitted, since the heavens would have regarded it as the pit of Babel:

> What are you building?—I want to dig a subterranean passage. Some progress must be made. My station up there is much too high.
> We are digging the pit of Babel.

Bannadonna is closest to the most extraordinary of the Kafkan parables concerning the Tower, in which a scholar maintains that the Great Wall of China "alone would provide for the first time in the history of mankind a secure foundation for the new Tower of Babel. First the wall, therefore, and then the tower." The final sentence of "The Great Wall and the Tower of Babel" could have impressed Melville as the best possible commentary upon Bannadonna-Melville, both in his project and his fate:

> There were many wild ideas in people's heads at that time—this scholar's book is only one example—perhaps simply because so many were trying to join forces as far as they could for the achievement of a single aim. Human nature, essentially changeable, unstable as the dust, can endure no restraint; if it binds itself it soon begins to tear madly at its bonds, until it rends everything asunder, the wall, the bonds and its very self.

The fall of Bannadonna commences with the casting of the great bell:

> The unleashed metals bayed like hounds. The workmen shrunk. Through their fright, fatal harm to the bell was dreaded. Fearless as Shadrach, Bannadonna, rushing through the glow, smote the chief culprit with his ponderous ladle. From the smitten part, a splinter was dashed into the seething mass, and at once was melted in.

That single blemish is evidently Melville's personal allegory for whatever sense of guilt, in his own pained judgment, flawed his own achievement, even in *Moby-Dick*. More interesting is Bannadonna's creation of a kind of *golem* or Frankensteinean monster, charmingly called Haman, doubtless in tribute to the villain of the Book of Esther. Haman, intended to be the bell-ringer, is meant also "as a partial type of an ulterior creature," a titanic helot who would be called Talus, like the rather sinister iron man who wields an iron flail against the rebellious Irish in the savage book 5 of Spenser's *The Faerie Queene*. But Talus is never created; Haman is quite enough to immolate the ambitious artist, Bannadonna:

> And so, for the interval, he was oblivious of his creature; which, not oblivious of him, and true to its creation, and true to its heedful winding up, left its post precisely at the given moment; along its well-oiled route, slid noiselessly towards its mark; and, aiming at the hand of Una, to ring one clangorous note, dully smote the intervening brain of Bannadonna, turned backwards to it; the manacled arms then instantly up-springing to their hovering poise. The falling body clogged the thing's return; so there it stood, still impending over Bannadonna, as if

whispering some post-mortem terror. The chisel lay dropped from the hand, but beside the hand; the oil-flask spilled across the iron track.

Which of his own works destroyed Melville? Juxtapose the story's deliberately Addisonian or Johnsonian conclusion with the remarkable stanza in Hart Crane's "The Broken Tower" that it helped inspire, and perhaps a hint emerges, since Crane was a superb interpreter of Melville:

> So the blind slave obeyed its blinder lord; but, in obedience, slew him. So the creator was killed by the creature. So the bell was too heavy for the tower. So that bell's main weakness was where man's blood had flawed it. And so pride went before the fall.

> The bells, I say, the bells break down their tower;
> And swing I know not where. Their tongues engrave
> Membrane through marrow, my long-scattered score
> Of broken intervals ... And I, their sexton slave!

Crane is both Bannadonna and Haman, a complex fate darker even than Melville's, who certainly had represented himself as Bannadonna. The Bell-Tower of Bannadonna perhaps was Pierre but more likely *Moby-Dick* itself, Melville's "long-scattered score / Of broken intervals" even as *The Bridge* was Hart Crane's. This is hardly to suggest that Haman is Captain Ahab. Yet Melville's "wicked book," as he called *Moby-Dick* in a famous letter to Hawthorne, indeed may have slain something vital in its author, if only in his retrospective consciousness.

Lewis Carroll

(1832-1898)

"And yet what a dear little puppy it was!" said Alice, as she leant against a buttercup to rest herself, and fanned herself with one of the leaves. "I should have liked teaching it tricks very much, if—if I'd only been the right size to do it! Oh dear! I'd nearly forgotten that I've got to grow up again!"

WHATEVER THE PROCESS IS OF RENEWING ONE'S EXPERIENCE OF *ALICE'S Adventures in Wonderland, Through the Looking-Glass*, and *The Hunting of the Snark*, the sensation is neither that of rereading nor of reading as though for the first time. Lewis Carroll is Shakespearean to the degree that his writing has become a kind of Scripture for us. Take, quite at random, the sublimely outrageous chapter 6, "Pig and Pepper," of *Alice's Adventures in Wonderland*. Alice enters a large, smoky kitchen and discovers an atmosphere permeated with pepper, a sneezing Duchess, and a howling and sneezing baby, as well as a cook stirring a cauldron of soup, and a large, grinning Cheshire Cat. Carroll's prevalent phantasmagoria heightens (if that is possible) as the cook commences to throw everything within her reach (fire-irons, saucepans, dishes) at the Duchess and her howling imp, while the Duchess cries out: "Chop off her head!" and sings a sort of lullaby to her baby, thoughtfully shaking it (violently) at the end of each line:

"Speak roughly to your little boy,
    And beat him when he sneezes:
He only does it to annoy,
    Because he knows it teases."

CHORUS
(in which the cook and the baby joined):—

42

"Wow! wow! wow!"

While the Duchess sang the second verse of the song, she kept tossing the baby violently up and down, and the poor little thing howled so, that Alice could hardly hear the words:—

"I speak severely to my boy,
    And beat him when he sneezes:
For he can thoroughly enjoy
    The pepper when he pleases!"

CHORUS
"Wow! wow! wow!"

"Here! You may nurse it a bit, if you like!" the Duchess said to Alice, flinging the baby at her as she spoke. "I must go and get ready to play croquet with the Queen," and she hurried out of the room. The cook threw a frying-pan after her as she went, but it just missed her.

Carroll stated the parodist's principle as choosing the best poems for model, but here the paradigm is a ghastly children's poem of the mid-nineteenth century:

Speak gently to the little child!
    Its love be sure to gain;
Teach it in accents soft and mild;
    It may not long remain.

That is ghastly enough to be its own parody, but Carroll wants it for his own dark purposes. The pepper is peculiarly analogous to a sexual stimulant, and the boy baby turns out to be a pig (presumably because little boys were not the objects of Carroll's affections). Alice, like Carroll, has no use for them:

So she set the little creature down, and felt quite relieved to see it trot away quietly into the wood. "If it had grown up," she said to herself, "it would have made a dreadfully ugly child: but it makes rather a handsome pig, I think." And she began thinking over other children she knew, who might do very well as pigs, and was just saying to herself, "if one only knew the right way to change them—" when she was a little startled by seeing the Cheshire Cat sitting on a bough of a tree a few yards off.

The Cheshire Cat is an ironic enigma, typical of many such in Carroll's enigmatic or riddling allegory. He is thoroughly unpleasant, but so, generally, are many of the inhabitants of Wonderland. It is a truism of criticism to remark that the child Alice is considerably more mature than any of the inhabitants of Wonderland, but what the Cheshire Cat remarks is true also:

> The Cat only grinned when it saw Alice. It looked good-natured, she thought: still it had very long claws and a great many teeth, so she felt that it ought to be treated with respect.
>
> "Cheshire Puss," she began, rather timidly, as she did not at all know whether it would like the name: however, it only grinned a little wider. "Come, it's pleased so far," thought Alice, and she went on. "Would you tell me, please, which way I ought to go from here?"
>
> "That depends a good deal on where you want to get to," said the Cat.
>
> "I don't much care where—" said Alice.
>
> "Then it doesn't matter which way you go," said the Cat.
>
> "—so long as I get *somewhere*," Alice added as an explanation.
>
> "Oh, you're sure to do that," said the Cat, "if you only walk long enough."
>
> Alice felt that this could not be denied, so she tried another question. "What sort of people live about here?"
>
> "In *that* direction," the Cat said, waving its right paw round, "lives a Hatter: and in *that* direction," waving the other paw, "lives a March Hare. Visit either you like: they're both mad."
>
> "But I don't want to go among mad people," Alice remarked.
>
> "Oh, you can't help that," said the Cat: "we're all mad here. I'm mad. You're mad."
>
> "How do you know I'm mad?" said Alice.
>
> "You must be," said the Cat, "or you wouldn't have come here."
>
> Alice didn't think that proved it at all: however, she went on: "And how do you know that you're mad?"
>
> "To begin with," said the Cat, "a dog's not mad. You grant that?"
>
> "I suppose so," said Alice.
>
> "Well, then," the Cat went on, "you see a dog growls when it's angry, and wags its tail when it's pleased. Now *I* growl when

I'm pleased, and wag my tail when I'm angry. Therefore I'm mad."

"*I* call it purring, not growling," said Alice.

Is Alice mad, because she has come to Wonderland? When the Cheshire Cat reappears, it stages a famously slow vanishing, ending with its grin, which stays on for some time after the rest of it is gone. That ontological grin is the emblem of the Cheshire Cat's madness, and is the prelude to the Mad Tea Party of the next chapter, which in turn is emblematical of the *Alice* books, since they can be described, quite accurately, as a mad tea party, rather than a nonsensical tea party. Lionel Trilling spoke of "the world of nonsense, that curious invention of the English of the nineteenth century, of Lewis Carroll and Edward Lear," and confessed that, critically, nonsense seemed to him inexplicable: "One of the mysteries of art, perhaps as impenetrable as why tragedy gives pleasure, is why nonsense commands so fascinated an attention, and why, when it succeeds, it makes more than sense."

A critic as distinguished as Trilling, William Empson, sought to solve the mystery by finding a defense against madness in Alice's characteristic stance:

> Much of the technique of the rudeness of the Mad Hatter has been learned from Hamlet. It is the ground-bass of this kinship with insanity, I think, that makes it so clear that the books are not trifling, and the cool courage with which Alice accepts madmen that gives them their strength.
> ("The Child as Swain," *Some Versions of Pastoral*)

It does not seem to me either that Carroll makes nonsense into "more than sense" or that Alice's undoubted courage is particularly cool. Unlike the sublime Edward Lear, Carroll does not read to me as a nonsense writer. Riddle is not nonsense, and enigmatic allegory does not exalt courage as the major virtue. Carroll is a Victorian Romantic just as were his exact contemporaries, the Pre-Raphaelite poets, but his phantasmagoria, utterly unlike theirs, is a wholly successful defense against, or revision of, High Romantic Quest. Christina Rossetti's *Goblin Market* has more in common with Edward Lear than Carroll does, and Swinburne is an even defter parodist than Carroll.

Carroll's parodies, sometimes brilliant though they are, do not transcend their echoes, do not reverse Carroll's own burden of literary belatedness. But the *Alice* books and *The Hunting of the Snark* do achieve convincing originality, while the Pre-Raphaelites sometimes are merely involuntary parodies of Keats, Shelley, Tennyson, and Browning. Romantic erotic quest, which ends in the Inferno of Shelley's *The Triumph of Life*, is displaced into the purgatorial sadomasochism of the Pre-Raphaelite poets. Dante Gabriel Rossetti, Swinburne, and their critical follower, Pater, substitute or trope the body for time, and accept the violence of the will's revenge against time upon their own bodies.

Carroll evades both sadomasochism and the Romantic erotic quest by identifying himself with the seven-year-old Alice. Wonderland has only one reality principle, which is that time has been murdered. Nothing need be substituted for time, even though only madness can murder time. Alice is only as mad as she needs to be, which may be her actual legacy from Hamlet. She will not grow up, or sexually mature, so long as she can get back into Wonderland, and she can get back out of Wonderland whenever she needs to. The Pre-Raphaelites and Pater are immersed in the world of the reality principle, the world of Schopenhauer and Freud. Psychoanalytic interpretations of Carroll's works always fail, because they are necessarily easy and vulgar, and therefore disgusting. Alice does not deign to be told what she is evading, and Carroll's books are not exercises in sublimation. What is repressed in them is his discomfort with culture, including Wordsworth, the largest precursor of his vision.

II

> "Hold your tongue!" said the Queen, turning purple.
> "I won't!" said Alice.
> "Off with her head!" the Queen shouted at the top of her voice. Nobody moved.
> "Who cares for you?" said Alice (she had grown to her full size by this time). "You're nothing but a pack of cards!"

This is the crisis of *Alice's Adventures in Wonderland*; it asserts Alice's freedom from her own phantasmagoria, after which she returns to our order of reality. The parallel moment in *Through the Looking-Glass* is a weak repetition of this splendor:

> There was not a moment to be lost. Already several of the guests were lying down in the dishes, and the soup-ladle was walking up the table towards Alice's chair, and beckoning to her impatiently to get out of its way.
> "I can't stand this any longer!" she cried, as she jumped up and seized the tablecloth with both hands: one good pull, and

plates, dishes, guests, and candles came crashing down together in a heap on the floor.

The movement from "You're nothing but a pack of cards!" to "I can't stand this any longer!" is a fair representation of the relative aesthetic decline the reader experiences as she goes from *Alice's Adventures in Wonderland* to *Through the Looking-Glass*. Had the first book never existed, our regard for the second would be unique and immense, which is only another way of admiring how the first *Alice* narrative is able to avoid any human affect as mundane as bitterness. The White Rabbit is an extraordinary parody of Carroll's own sense of literary and even erotic belatedness, yet the quality he conveys is an exuberant vivacity. We are, all of us, now perpetually late for a very important date, but that apprehension of being late, late is for many among us an anxious expectation. For Carroll, in his first vision as Alice, everything is again early, which gives the book its pure and radiant atmosphere of a triumphant fastness.

Bitterness keeps breaking in as we read *Through the Looking-Glass*, which may explain how weirdly and perpetually contemporary this second and somewhat lesser work now seems. Its epitome is that grand poem, "The Walrus and the Carpenter":

> "'But wait a bit,' the Oysters cried,
>   'Before we have our chat;
> For some of us are out of breath,
>   And all of us are fat!'
> 'No hurry!' said the Carpenter.
>   They thanked him much for that.
>
> 'A loaf of bread,' the Walrus said,
>   'Is what we chiefly need:
> Pepper and vinegar besides
>   Are very good indeed—
> Now, if you're ready, Oysters dear,
>   We can begin to feed.'
>
> 'But not on us!' the Oysters cried,
>   Turning a little blue.
> 'After such kindness, that would be
>   A dismal thing to do!'
> 'The night is fine,' the Walrus said.
>   'Do you admire the view?

'It was so kind of you to come!
   And you are very nice!'
The Carpenter said nothing but
   'Cut us another slice.
I wish you were not quite so deaf—
   I've had to ask you twice!'

'It seems a shame,' the Walrus said,
   'To play them such a trick.
After we've brought them out so far,
   And made them trot so quick!'
The Carpenter said nothing but
   'The butter's spread too thick!'

'I weep for you,' the Walrus said:
   'I deeply sympathize.'
With sobs and tears he sorted out
   Those of the largest size,
Holding his pocket-handkerchief
   Before his streaming eyes.

'O Oysters,' said the Carpenter,
   'You've had a pleasant run!
Shall we be trotting home again?'
   But answer came there none—
And this was scarcely odd, because
   They'd eaten every one."

In an additional stanza, written for a theatrical presentation of the *Alice* narratives, but fortunately not part of our received text, Carroll accuses the Walrus and the Carpenter of "craft and cruelty," a judgment in which Alice joins him when she remarks that "They were *both* very unpleasant characters—." But so are the Sheep, and that pompous egghead Humpty Dumpty, though we do not receive them as quite the weird representations that actually they indeed constitute. Carroll's art renders each of them as totally idiosyncratic, it being Carroll's largest enigma that only Alice, in either book, lacks personality or pathos. In "The Walrus and the Carpenter," those two voracious deceivers are neatly distinguished from one another. They are both weepers, high Victorian sentimentalists, living in a contra-natural midnight world where the sun outshines the sulky moon, presumably an indication that this world oddly is natural—all-too-natural—which is to say: hungry.

The Walrus and the Carpenter weep to increase their appetites, as it were, but the Walrus, being the orator of the two, is finally so moved by his own eloquence that he weeps on, even when he is happily satiated. Though he is more cunning than the Carpenter, he is also less sadistic; we wince a bit at the Carpenter's "Shall we be trotting home again?" but we ought to wince more when the Walrus sobbingly says: "I weep for you. I deeply sympathize."

Humpty Dumpty may well be Carroll's most famous enigma, and his most Shakespearean. He is also a prophecy of many of our contemporary literary theorists: "I can explain all the poems that ever were invented—and a good many that haven't been invented just yet." "You're so exactly like other people," Humpty Dumpty rather nastily says to Alice, but he receives his comeuppance just as she pronounces her accurate normative judgment that he is truly "unsatisfactory."

The White Knight, at once the most satisfactory and charmingly pleasant of Carroll's enigmas, is the figure in *Through the Looking-Glass* who returns us vividly to the gentler spirit of *Alice's Adventurer in Wonderland*. There is a critical tradition that the White Knight is a self-portrait of Charles Lutwidge Dodgson, the other self of Lewis Carroll in the world of the reality principle. There may be something to this, but more palpably the White Knight is a version of the kindly, heroic, and benignly mad Don Quixote. The White Knight's madness is like Alice's own malady, if the Cheshire Cat was right about Alice. It is the madness of play, Carroll's sweet madness, a defense against darker madness.

Carroll's best poem ever is "The White Knight's Ballad," which is a superb and loving parody of Wordsworth's great crisis-poem "Resolution and Independence." Wordsworth's near-solipsism, his inability to listen to what the old Leech-gatherer is saying in answer to the poet's anguished question ("How is it that you live, and what is it you do?") was mocked rather mercilessly in Carroll's original version of his poem, published in 1856, fifteen years before *Through the Looking-Glass*. In the 1856 poem, "Upon the Lonely Moor," the poet is outrageously rough and even brutal to the aged man, who is not just unheard but is kicked, punched, boxed on the ear, and has his hair tweaked. All this happily is softened in the beautiful revision that is the song sung by the White Knight:

> "It's long," said the Knight, "but it's very, *very* beautiful. Everybody that hears me sing it—either it brings the tears into their eyes, or else—"
> "Or else what?" said Alice, for the Knight had made a sudden pause.

"Or else it doesn't, you know. The name of the song is called *'Haddocks' Eyes.'*"

"Oh, that's the name of the song, is it?" Alice said, trying to feel interested.

"No, you don't understand," the Knight said, looking a little vexed. "That's what the name is *called*. The name really is *'The Aged Aged Man .'*"

"Then I ought to have said 'That's what the *song* is called'?" Alice corrected herself.

"No, you oughtn't: that's quite another thing! The *song* is called *'Ways And Means'*: but that's only what it's *called*, you know!"

"Well, what *is* the song, then?" said Alice, who was by this time completely bewildered.

"I was coming to that," the Knight said. "The song really it *'A-sitting On A Gate'*: and the tune's my own invention."

So saying, he stopped his horse and let the reins fall on its neck: then, slowly beating time with one hand, and with a faint smile lighting up his gentle foolish face, as if he enjoyed the music of his song, he began.

Of all the strange things that Alice saw in her journey Through The Looking-Glass, this was the one that she always remembered most clearly. Years afterwards she could bring the whole scene back again, as if it had been only yesterday—the mild blue eyes and kindly smile of the Knight—the setting sun gleaming through his hair, and shining on his armour in a blaze of light that quite dazzled her—the horse quietly moving about, with the reins hanging loose on his neck, cropping the grass at her feet—and the black shadows of the forest behind—all this she took in like a picture, as, with one hand shading her eyes, she leant against a tree, watching the strange pair, and listening, in a half-dream, to the melancholy music of the song.

"But the tune *isn't* his own invention," she said to herself: "it's *'I give thee all, I can no more.'*" She stood and listened very attentively, but no tears came into her eyes.

"I'll tell thee everything I can:
　　There's little to relate.
I saw an aged aged man,
　　A-sitting on a gate.
'Who are you, aged man?' I said.

'And how is it you live?'
And his answer trickled through my head,
    Like water through a sieve.

He said 'I look for butterflies
    That sleep among the wheat:
I make them into mutton-pies,
    And sell them in the street.
I sell them unto men,' he said,
    'Who sail on stormy seas;
And that's the way I get my bread—
    A trifle, if you please.'

But I was thinking of a plan
    To dye one's whiskers green,
And always use so large a fan
    That they could not be seen.
So, having no reply to give
    To what the old man said,
I cried 'Come, tell me how you live!'
    And thumped him on the head.

His accents mild took up the tale:
    He said 'I go my ways,
And when I find a mountain-rill,
    I set it in a blaze;
And thence they make a stuff they call
    Rowland's Macassar-Oil—
Yet twopence-halfpenny is all
    They give me for my toil.'

But I was thinking of a way
    To feed oneself on batter,
And so go on from day to day
    Getting a little fatter.
I shook him well from side to side,
    Until his face was blue:
'Come, tell me how you live,' I cried,
    'And what it is you do!'

He said 'I hunt for haddocks' eyes

Among the heather bright,
And work them into waistcoat—
    buttons
In the silent night.
And these I do not sell for gold
    Or coin of silvery shine,
But for a copper halfpenny,
    And that will purchase nine.'"

Thumped and shaken blue, but otherwise undamaged, the aged hunter for haddocks' eyes is a belated but less fearful representative of the reality principle than Wordsworth's Leech-gatherer. As much as the Leech-gatherer, the White Knight's decrepit survivor is "like a man from some far region sent, / To give me human strength, by apt admonishment." The alternative for Carroll, as for Wordsworth, would be despondency and madness, the waning of the poet's youthful joy into a death-in-life. But Carroll, fiercely defending against his own Wordsworthianism, triumphantly makes it new in a final vision of the aged man that is anything but Wordsworthian, because it is pure Wonderland:

"And now, if e'er by chance I put
    My fingers into glue,
Or madly squeeze a right-hand foot
    Into a left-hand shoe,
Or if I drop upon my toe
    A very heavy weight,
I weep, for it reminds me so
Of that old man I used to know—
Whose look was mild, whose speech
    was slow,
Whose hair was whiter than the snow,
Whose face was very like a crow,
With eyes, like cinders, all aglow,
Who seemed distracted with his woe,
Who rocked his body to and fro,
And muttered mumblingly and low,
As if his mouth were full of dough,
Who snorted like a buffalo—
That summer evening long ago,
    A-sitting on a gate."

Mark Twain

(1835-1910)

THE MOST USEFUL CRITICAL STUDY OF MARK TWAIN, FOR ME, REMAINS James M. Cox's *Mark Twain: The Fate of Humor* (1966). Cox does not deal with the short stories but rather with Twain's major works, including *Adventures of Huckleberry Finn, Pudd'nhead Wilson, Roughing It*, and *Innocents Abroad*. It is Cox who points out that "Mark Twain" was a steamboat pilot's signal for danger, not for safe water. Samuel Clemens, who became Mark Twain, remains our leading humorist, but his best work—the short stories included—is replete with signals for danger. Cox emphasizes also the recurrence in Twain's writings of the figure of a Stranger—ironic and mysterious—whose interventions bring about danger, whether to the established moral order or to our universal lust for illusions.

Twain, in Cox's view, fought a lifelong campaign against the censorious conscience, the Freudian superego. A speculator by nature, Twain was a great escape artist, like his masterly creation, Huck Finn. The best of Twain's short stories are exercises in evasiveness, because the truth, as for Hamlet, is what kills us. The abyss of nihilism beckons as uncannily in Mark Twain as it does in Shakespeare, or in Nietzsche.

Twain's first artistic and commercial success was his early short story (1865), "The Celebrated Jumping Frog of Calaveras County," where the storyteller, Wheeler, is the ancestor of all the deadpan narrators who are the glory of Twain's style. Twain became one of the great performers of his age; his lectures, mock-solemnly delivered, vied in effectiveness with Emerson's visionary addresses and Dickens's dramatic readings. Wheeler's mode of narration became Twain's platform manner: disarmingly innocent and yet comically urgent.

In 1876, Twain read aloud, to a select Hartford audience, the outrageous "Facts concerning the Recent Carnival of Crime in Connecticut," a fantasy in which the ironic dwarf, his Conscience, is destroyed by the narrator as prelude to beginning the world anew:

> I killed thirty-eight persons during the first two weeks—all of them on account of ancient grudges. I burned a dwelling that interrupted my view. I swindled a widow and some orphans out of their last cow ...

The war against the superego is carried on much more indirectly in "The Stolen White Elephant" of 1882, where the parody of detective-fiction hyperbolically indicts what might be termed the investigative impulse itself. A fear of madness, at the root of Twain's genius for humor, translated into the superb story, "The Man That Corrupted Hadleyburg," a *Paradise Lost*-in-little, with intimations of Pre-Millennialism (1899). Hadleyburg, "the most honest and upright little town in all the region round about," could be anywhere in the United States as we again approach the Millennium. The man who "corrupts" it is an archetypal Mark Twain mysterious or ironic Stranger, a truth-seeking Satan. A small masterpiece in style and plot, the Fall of Hadleyburg may be Twain's finest victory over the hypocrisies of the societal element in the superego.

With "The £1,000,000 Note" of 1893, Twain refined his parable of corruption. Light as this story continues to be, it has few peers in its revelation of the illusions of finance. Nihilism, a Gnostic awareness of the illusiveness of both nature and society, attains its extreme of intensity in the posthumously published *Mysterious Stranger* fragments. Little Satan, Twain's final hero, indicts the superego or Moral Sense as the true villain of human existence. God, the deity of Moral Virtue akin to Blake's Urizen, is the final culprit, for Mark Twain. An attack upon God, however God is construed, is a very difficult basis for humor, as Twain realized. At the outer limits of his art, Twain yielded to despair.

Henry James

(1843–1916)

THE INTENSE CRITICAL ADMIRERS OF HENRY JAMES GO SO FAR AS TO CALL him the major American writer, or even the most accomplished novelist in the English language. The first assertion neglects only Walt Whitman, while the second partly evades the marvelous sequence that moves from Samuel Richardson's *Clarissa* through Jane Austen on to George Eliot, and the alternative tradition that goes from Fielding through Dickens to Joyce. James is certainly the crucial American novelist, and in his best works the true peer of Austen and George Eliot. His precursor, Hawthorne, is more than fulfilled in the splendors of *The Portrait of a Lady* and *The Wings of the Dove*, giant descendants of *The Marble Faun*, while the rival American novelists—Melville, Mark Twain, Dreiser, Faulkner—survive comparison with James only by being so totally unlike him. Unlikeness makes Faulkner—particularly in his great phase—a true if momentary rival, and perhaps if you are to find a non-Jamesian sense of sustained power in the American novel, you need to seek out our curious antithetical tradition that moves between *Moby-Dick* and its darker descendants: *As I Lay Dying*, *Miss Lonelyhearts*, *The Crying of Lot 49*. The normative consciousness of our prose fiction, first prophesied by *The Scarlet Letter*, was forged by Henry James, whose spirit lingers not only in palpable disciples like Edith Wharton in *The Age of Innocence* and Willa Cather in her superb *A Lost Lady*, but more subtly (because merged with Joseph Conrad's aura) in novelists as various as Fitzgerald, Hemingway, and Warren. It seems clear that the relation of James to American prose fiction is precisely analogous to Whitman's relation to our poetry; each is, in his own sphere, what Emerson prophesied as the Central Man who would come and change all things forever, in a celebration of the American Newness.

The irony of James's central position among our novelists is palpable, since, like the much smaller figure of T.S. Eliot later on, James abandoned his nation and eventually became a British subject, after having been born a citizen in Emerson's America. But it is a useful commonplace of criticism that James remained the most American of novelists, not less peculiarly nationalistic in *The Ambassadors* than he had been in "Daisy Miller" and *The American*. James, a subtle if at times perverse literary critic, understood very well what we continue to learn and relearn; an American writer can be Emersonian or anti-Emersonian, but even a negative stance towards Emerson always leads back again to his formulation of the post-Christian American religion of Self-Reliance. Overt Emersonians like Thoreau, Whitman, and Frost are no more pervaded by the Sage of Concord than are anti-Emersonians like Hawthorne, Melville, and Eliot. Perhaps the most haunted are those writers who evade Emerson, yet never leave his dialectical ambiance, a group that includes Emily Dickinson, Henry James, and Wallace Stevens.

Emerson was for Henry James something of a family tradition, though that in itself hardly accounts for the plain failure of very nearly everything that the novelist wrote about the essayist. James invariably resorts to a tone of ironic indulgence on the subject of Emerson, which is hardly appropriate to the American prophet of Power, Fate, Illusions, and Wealth. I suggest that James unknowingly mixed Emerson up with the sage's good friend Henry James, Sr., whom we dismiss as a Swedenborgian, but who might better be characterized as an American Gnostic speculator, in Emerson's mode, though closer in eminence to, say, Bronson Alcott than to the author of *The Conduct of Life*.

The sane and sacred Emerson was a master of evasions, particularly when disciples became too pressing, whether upon personal or spiritual matters. The senior Henry James is remembered now for having fathered Henry, William, and Alice, and also for his famous outburst against Emerson, whom he admired on the other side of idolatry: "O you man without a handle!"

The junior Henry James, overtly celebrating Emerson, nevertheless remarked: "It is hardly too much, or too little, to say of Emerson's writings in general that they were not composed at all." "Composed" is the crucial word there, and makes me remember a beautiful moment in Stevens's "The Poems of Our Climate":

> There would still remain the never-resting mind,
> So that one would want to escape, come back
> To what had been so long composed.

Emerson's mind, never merely restless, indeed was never-resting, as was the mind of every member of the James family. The writings of Emerson, not composed at all, constantly come back to what had been so long composed, to what his admirer Nietzsche called the primordial poem of mankind, the fiction that we have knocked together and called our cosmos. James was far too subtle not to have known this. He chose not to know it, because he needed a provincial Emerson even as he needed a provincial Hawthorne, just as he needed a New England that never was: simple, gentle, and isolated, even a little childlike.

The days when T.S. Eliot could wonder why Henry James had not carved up R.W. Emerson seem safely past, but we ought to remember Eliot's odd complaint about James as critic: "Even in handling men whom he could, one supposes, have carved joint from joint—Emerson or Norton—his touch is uncertain; there is a desire to be generous, a political motive, an admission (in dealing with American writers) that under the circumstances this was the best possible, or that it has fine qualities." Aside from appearing to rank Emerson with Charles Eliot Norton (which is comparable to ranking Freud with Bernard Berenson), this unamiable judgment reduces Emerson, who was and is merely the mind of America, to the stature of a figure who might, at most, warrant the condescension of James (and of Eliot). The cultural polemic involved is obvious, and indeed obsessive, in Eliot, but though pleasanter in James is really no more acceptable:

> Of the three periods into which his life divides itself, the first was (as in the case of most men) that of movement, experiment and selection—that of effort too and painful probation. Emerson had his message, but he was a good while looking for his form—the form which, as he himself would have said, he never completely found and of which it was rather characteristic of him that his later years (with their growing refusal to give him the *word*), wishing to attack him in his most vulnerable point, where his tenure was least complete, had in some degree the effect of despoiling him. It all sounds rather bare and stern, Mr. Cabot's account of his youth and early manhood, and we get an impression of a terrible paucity of alternatives. If he would be neither a farmer nor a trader he could "teach school"; that was the main resource and a part of the general educative process of the young New Englander who proposed to devote himself to the things of the mind. There was an advantage in the nudity, however, which was that, in Emerson's case at least,

the things of the mind did get themselves admirably well considered. If it be his great distinction and his special sign that he had a more vivid conception of the moral life than any one else, it is probably not fanciful to say that he owed it in part to the limited way in which he saw our capacity for living illustrated. The plain, God-fearing, practical society which surrounded him was not fertile in variations: it had great intelligence and energy, but it moved altogether in the straightforward direction. On three occasions later—three journeys to Europe—he was introduced to a more complicated world; but his spirit, his moral taste, as it were, abode always within the undecorated walls of his youth. There he could dwell with that ripe unconsciousness of evil which is one of the most beautiful signs by which we know him. His early writings are full of quaint animadversion upon the vices of the place and time, but there is something charmingly vague, light and general in the arraignment. Almost the worst he can say is that these vices are negative and that his fellow-townsmen are not heroic. We feel that his first impressions were gathered in a community from which misery and extravagance, and either extreme, of any sort, were equally absent. What the life of New England fifty years ago offered to the observer was the common lot, in a kind of achromatic picture, without particular intensifications. It was from this table of the usual, the merely typical joys and sorrows that he proceeded to generalise—a fact that accounts in some degree for a certain inadequacy and thinness in his enumerations. But it helps to account also for his direct, intimate vision of the soul itself—not in its emotions, its contortions and perversions, but in its passive, exposed, yet healthy form. He knows the nature of man and the long tradition of its dangers; but we feel that whereas he can put his finger on the remedies, lying for the most part, as they do, in the deep recesses of virtue, of the spirit, he has only a kind of hearsay, uninformed acquaintance with the disorders. It would require some ingenuity, the reader may say too much, to trace closely this correspondence between his genius and the frugal, dutiful, happy but decidedly lean Boston of the past, where there was a great deal of will but very little fulcrum—like a ministry without an opposition.

The genius itself it seems to me impossible to contest—I mean the genius for seeing character as a real and supreme thing. Other writers have arrived at a more complete expression: Wordsworth and Goethe, for instance, give one a sense of having found their form, whereas with Emerson we never lose the sense that he is still seeking it. But no one has had so steady and constant, and above all so natural, a vision of what we require and what we are capable of in the way of aspiration and independence. With Emerson it is ever the special capacity for moral experience—always that and only that. We have the impression, somehow, that life had never bribed him to look at anything but the soul; and indeed in the world in which he grew up and lived the bribes and lures, the beguilements and prizes, were few. He was in an admirable position for showing, what he constantly endeavoured to show, that the prize was within. Any one who in New England at that time could do that was sure of success, of listeners and sympathy: most of all, of course, when it was a question of doing it with such a divine persuasiveness. Moreover, the way in which Emerson did it added to the charm—by word of mouth, face to face, with a rare, irresistible voice and a beautiful mild, modest authority. If Mr. Arnold is struck with the limited degree in which he was a man of letters I suppose it is because he is more struck with his having been, as it were, a man of lectures. But the lecture surely was never more purged of its grossness—the quality in it that suggests a strong light and a big brush—than as it issued from Emerson's lips; so far from being a vulgarisation, it was simply the esoteric made audible, and instead of treating the few as the many, after the usual fashion of gentlemen on platforms, he treated the many as the few. There was probably no other society at that time in which he would have got so many persons to understand that; for we think the better of his audience as we read him, and wonder where else people would have had so much moral attention to give. It is to be remembered however that during the winter of 1847–48, on the occasion of his second visit to England, he found many listeners in London and in provincial cities. Mr. Cabot's volumes are full of evidence of the satisfactions he offered, the delights and revelations he may be said to have promised, to a race which had to seek its entertainment, its rewards and consolations, almost exclusively in the moral world. But his own writings are fuller still; we find an instance almost wherever we open them.

It is astonishing to me that James judged Emerson's "great distinction" and "special sign" to be "that he had a more vivid conception of the moral life than anyone else," unless "the moral life" has an altogether Jamesian meaning. I would rather say that the great distinction and special sign of James's fiction is that it represents a more vivid conception of the moral life than even Jane Austen or George Eliot could convey to us. Emerson is not much more concerned with morals than he is with manners; his subjects are power, freedom, and fate. As for "that ripe unconsciousness of evil" that James found in Emerson, I have not been able to find it myself, after reading Emerson almost daily for the last twenty years, and I am reminded of Yeats's late essay on Shelley's *Prometheus Unbound*, in which Yeats declares that his skeptical and passionate precursor, great poet that he certainly was, necessarily lacked the Vision of Evil. The necessity in both strong mis-readings, James's and Yeats's, was to clear more space for themselves.

Jealous as I am for Emerson, I can recognize that no critic has matched James in seeing and saying what Emerson's strongest virtue is: "But no one has had so steady and constant, and above all so natural, a vision of what we require and what we are capable of in the way of aspiration and independence." No one, that is, except Henry James, for that surely is the quest of Isabel Archer towards her own quite Emersonian vision of aspiration and independence. "The moral world" is James's phrase and James's emphasis. Emerson's own emphasis, I suspect, was considerably more pragmatic than that of James. When James returned to America in 1904 on a visit, after twenty years of self-exile, he went back to Concord and recorded his impressions in *The American Scene*:

> It is odd, and it is also exquisite, that these witnessing ways should be the last ground on which we feel moved to ponderation of the "Concord school"—to use, I admit, a futile expression; or rather, I should doubtless say, it *would* be odd if there were not inevitably something absolute in the fact of Emerson's all but lifelong connection with them. We may smile a little as we "drag in" Weimar, but I confess myself, for my part, much more satisfied than not by our happy equivalent, "in American money," for Goethe and Schiller. The money is a potful in the second case as in the first, and if Goethe, in the one, represents the gold and Schiller the silver, I find (and quite putting aside any bimetallic prejudice) the same good relation in the other between Emerson and Thoreau. I open Emerson for the same benefit for which I open Goethe, the sense of moving in large

intellectual space, and that of the gush, here and there, out of the rock, of the crystalline cupful, in wisdom and poetry, in Wahrheit and Dichtung; and whatever I open Thoreau for (I needn't take space here for the good reasons) I open him oftener than I open Schiller. Which comes back to our feeling that the rarity of Emerson's genius, which has made him so, for the attentive peoples, the first, and the one really rare, American spirit in letters, couldn't have spent his career in a charming woody, watery place, for so long socially and typically and, above all, interestingly homogeneous, without an effect as of the communication to it of something ineffaceable. It was during his long span his immediate concrete, sufficient world; it gave him his nearest vision of life, and he drew half his images, we recognize, from the revolution of its seasons and the play of its manners. I don't speak of the other half, which he drew from elsewhere. It is admirably, to-day, as if we were still seeing these things *in* those images, which stir the air like birds, dim in the eventide, coming home to nest. If one had reached a "time of life" one had thereby at least heard him lecture; and not a russet leaf fell for me, while I was there, but fell with an Emersonian drop.

That is a beautiful study of the nostalgias and tells us, *contra* T.S. Eliot, what James's relation to Emerson actually was. We know how much that is essential in William James was quarried out of Emerson, particularly from the essay "Experience," which gave birth to Pragmatism. Henry James was not less indebted to Emerson than William James was. *The Portrait of a Lady* is hardly an Emersonian novel; perhaps *The Scarlet Letter* actually is closer to that. Yet Isabel Archer is Emerson's daughter, just as Lambert Strether is Emerson's heir. The Emersonian aura also lingers on even in the ghostly tales of Henry James.

II

My own favorite among James's nouvelles is "The Pupil" (1891), not a ghostly tale, yet still deeply (if dialectically) Emersonian. "The Pupil" comes between the culmination of the earlier James in *The Bostonians* and *The Princess Casamassima* (both 1886) and the middle James of *The Spoils of Poynton* and *What Maisie Knew* (both 1897), and *The Awkward Age* (1899). In some respects, "The Pupil" seems to me the perfection in shorter form of James's earlier mode even as *The Portrait of a Lady* is its perfection on a full scale. Yet "The Pupil" is an enigmatic tale, so nuanced that a single interpretation is unlikely ever to gain wide credence.

In his "Preface to the New York Edition," James is suitably remote on 7 the actual moral drama enacted in "The Pupil." Writing on *What Maisie Knew*, James remarks that: "Small children have many more perceptions than they have terms to translate them; their vision is at any moment much richer, their apprehension even constantly stronger, than their prompt, their at all producible, vocabulary." Among Jamesian children, the tragic Morgan is the great exception to this principle; his preternaturally formidable vocabulary is invariably at the service of his accurate and comprehensive perceptions. Of Morgan, James affectionately observes: "My urchin of 'The Pupil' has sensibility in abundance; it would seem—and yet preserves in spite of it, I judge, his strong little male quality." It is certainly part of the story's immense charm that all of us, very quickly, come to share the author's (and Pemberton's) affection for Morgan, who is one of the grand portraits of the American as a young boy. I can think of no two American novelists of real eminence who shared as little as Henry James and Mark Twain, and yet I could imagine a conversation between Morgan Moreen and Huck Finn, two very different yet complementary images of the American boy longing for freedom.

In the only reference to Twain I can recall in James, the master rather nastily remarks (in 1874), that: "In the day of Mark Twain there is no harm in being reminded that the absence of drollery may, at a stretch, be compensated by the presence of sublimity." Well, James said far worse about Whitman and Dickens, and I myself prefer *Adventures of Huckleberry Finn* even to *The Portrait of a Lady*, but if we strip from James's observation its apotropaic gesture, we can grant that "The Pupil" abounds both in drollery and sublimity, even though clearly inferior to *Huckleberry Finn* in both qualities. Poor Morgan, very much a changeling in the Moreen family, would have benefited more even from Huck Finn as tutor than from Pemberton, if only Morgan had been robust enough to bear it.

There has been a critical fashion to blame the long-suffering and devoted Pemberton, as well as the outrageous Moreens, for Morgan's death, but this seems to me merely absurd. What after all could the penniless Pemberton, barely self-supporting even when free of the Moreens, have done with Morgan? The novella's final scene is exquisitely subtle, yet in my reading contains no abandonment of Morgan by Pemberton:

> "We've struggled, we've suffered," his wife went on; "but you've made him so your own that we've already been through the worst of the sacrifice."

Morgan had turned away from his father—he stood looking at Pemberton with a light in his face. His sense of shame for their common humiliated state had dropped; the case had another side—the thing was to clutch at *that*. He had a moment of boyish joy, scarcely mitigated by the reflexion that with this unexpected consecration of his hope—too sudden and too violent; the turn taken was away from a *good* boy's book—the "escape" was left on their hands. The boyish joy was there an instant, and Pemberton was almost scared at the rush of gratitude and affection that broke through his first abasement. When he stammered "My dear fellow, what do you say to *that*?" how could one not say something enthusiastic? But there was more need for courage at something else that immediately followed and that made the lad sit down quickly on the nearest chair. He had turned quite livid and had raised his hand to his left side. They were all three looking at him, but Mrs. Moreen suddenly bounded forward. "Ah his darling little heart!" she broke out; and this time, on her knees before him and without respect for the idol, she caught him ardently in her arms. "You walked him too far, you hurried him too fast!" she hurled over her shoulder at Pemberton. Her son made no protest, and the next instant, still holding him, she sprang up with her face convulsed and with the terrified cry "Help, help! he's going, he's gone!" Pemberton saw with equal horror, by Morgan's own stricken face, that he was beyond their wildest recall. He pulled him half out of his mother's hands, and for a moment, while they held him together, they looked all their dismay into each other's eyes. "He couldn't stand it with his weak organ," said Pemberton—"the shock, the whole scene, the violent emotion."

"But I thought he *wanted* to go to you!" wailed Mrs. Moreen.

"I *told* you he didn't, my dear," her husband made answer. Mr. Moreen was trembling all over and was in his way as deeply affected as his wife. But after the very first he took his bereavement as a man of the world.

Morgan, as I read it, dies not of grief at rejection, whether by the Moreens or Pemberton, but of excess of joy at the prospect of being taken away by Pemberton. This seems to me strikingly similar to the death of King Lear, since I agree with Harold Goddard's interpretation that Lear dies of joy rather than grief, in the hallucinated conviction that Cordelia's lips still move. What Yeats called "tragic joy" is a Shakespearean quality not easy to achieve, and it is extraordinary that James attains to that vision at the close of "The Pupil." But that still leaves us with the moral question concerning this great fiction; what could there have been for Morgan in a world so clearly inadequate to him?

James's beautiful (and false) objection to our father Emerson was that the sage had failed to achieve a style, and had to survive "on the strength of his message alone." I am hardly among those who find Emerson's message to be weak, but I know it to be strong primarily through and by his style. Wisdom has no authority for us unless and until it has individualized its rhetorical stance, and what preserves Emerson's shamanistic charisma is precisely his style. I find a touch, slight but definite, of that style in "The Pupil" which is nothing but an Emersonian parable of the fate of freedom or wildness in an alien context, which is to say, of the tragedy of the American spirit when it is taken into exile abroad, into the social perversions and false values of the Old World. James will not say so, in his "Preface," but Morgan is a victim of Europe, and of his family's vain attempt to domesticate itself in a realm where the Adamic stance has no proper place.

Read thus, "The Pupil" indeed becomes a sublime drollery, distant but authentic cousin to *Adventures of Huckleberry Finn*. Henry James, who finally became a subject of King George V, could not tolerate that admirable American writer, Mark Twain, who once deliciously suggested that the British ought to replace the House of Hanover by a medley of royal cats and kittens. But that did not prevent James from writing an involuntary self-chastisement in "The Pupil," an eloquent reprise of the Emersonian warning of the American fate if we did not face west into the evening-land, abandoning behind us the false dream of becoming men and women of the European world.

Guy de Maupassant

(1850–1893)

CHEKHOV HAD LEARNED FROM MAUPASSANT HOW TO REPRESENT BANALITY. Maupassant, who had learned everything, including that, from his master, Flaubert, rarely matches the genius of Chekhov, or Turgenev, as a story-teller. Lev Shestov, a remarkable Russian religious thinker of the earlier twentieth century, expressed this with considerable force:

> Chekhov's wonderful art did not die—his art to kill by a mere touch, a breath, a glance, everything whereby men live and wherein they take their pride. And in the art he was constantly perfecting himself, and he attained to a virtuosity beyond the reach of any of his rivals in European literature. Maupassant often had to strain every effort to overcome his victim. The victim often escaped from Maupassant, though crushed and broken, yet with his life. In Chekhov's hands, nothing escaped death.

That is a very dark view and no reader wants to think of herself as a writer's victim, and yet Shestov accurately weighs Maupassant against Chekhov, rather as one might weigh Christopher Marlowe against Shakespeare. Yet Maupassant is the best of the really "popular" story-writers, vastly superior to O. Henry (who could be quite good) and greatly preferable to the abominable Poe. To be an artist of the popular is itself an extraordinary achievement; we have nothing like it in the United States today.

Chekhov can seem simple, but is always profoundly subtle; many of Maupassant's simplicities are merely what they seem to be, yet they are not shallow. Maupassant had learned from his teacher Flaubert, that "talent is a prolonged patience" at seeing what others tend not to see. Whether Maupassant can make us see what we could never have seen without him, I very much doubt. That calls for the genius of Shakespeare, or of Chekhov. There is also the problem that Maupassant, like so many nineteenth- and early-twentieth-century writers of fiction, saw everything through the lens of Arthur Schopenhauer, philosopher of the Will-to-Live. I would just as soon wear Schopenhauerian as Freudian goggles; both enlarge and both distort, almost equally. But I am a literary critic, not a story-writer, and Maupassant would have done better to discard philosophical spectacles when he contemplated the vagaries of the desires of men and women.

At his best, he is marvelously readable, whether in the humorous pathos of "Madame Tellier's Establishment" or in a horror story like "The Horla," both of which I shall consider here. Frank O'Connor insisted that Maupassant's stories were not satisfactory when compared to those of Chekhov and Turgenev, but then few story-writers rival the two Russian masters. O'Connor's real objection was that he thought "the sexual act itself turns into a form of murder" in Maupassant. A reader who has just enjoyed "Madame Tellier's Establishment" would hardly agree. Flaubert, who did not live to write it, wished to set his final novel in a provincial whorehouse, which his son had already done in this robust story.

Everyone in "Madame Tellier's Establishment" is benign and amiable, which is part of the story's authentic charm. Madame Tellier, a respectable Norman peasant, keeps her establishment as one might run an inn or even a boarding school. Her five sex-workers (as some call them now) are vividly, even lovingly described by Madame's talent for conciliation, and her incessant good humor.

On an evening in May, none of the regular clients are in good humor, because the establishment is festooned with notice: CLOSED FOR A FIRST COMMUNION. Madame and her staff have gone off for this event, the celebrant being Madame's niece (and god-daughter). The First Communion develops into an extraordinary occasion when the prolonged weeping of the whores, moved to remember their own girlhoods, becomes contagious, and the entire congregation is swept by an ecstasy of tears. The priest proclaims that the Holy Christ has descended, and particularly thanks the visitors, Madame Tellier and her staff.

After a boisterous trip back to their establishment, Madame and her ladies return to their ordinary evening labors, performed however with more than the routine zest and in high good spirits. "It isn't every day we have something to celebrate," Madame Tellier concludes the story by remarking, and only a joyless reader declines to celebrate with her. For once, at least, Schopenhauer's disciple has broken loose from gloomy reflections on the close relations between sex and death.

Exuberance in storytelling is hard to resist, and Maupassant never writes with more gusto than in "Madame Tellier's Establishment." This tale of Normandy has warmth, laughter, surprise, and even a kind of spiritual insight. The Pentecostal ecstasy that burns through the congregation is as authentic as the weeping of the whores that ignites it. Maupassant's irony is markedly kinder (though less subtle) than his master Flaubert's. And the story is bawdy, not prurient, in the Shakespearean spirit; it enlarges life, and diminishes no one.

Maupassant's own life ended badly; by his late twenties, he was syphilitic. At thirty-nine, the disease affected his mind, and he spent his final years locked in an asylum, after a suicide attempt. His most upsetting horror story, "The Horla," has a complex and ambiguous relation to his illness and its consequences. The nameless protagonist of the story is perhaps a syphilitic going mad, though nothing that Maupassant narrates actually tells us to make such an inference. A first-person narration, "The Horla" gives us more clues than we can interpret, because we cannot understand the narrator, and do not know whether we can trust his impressions, of which we receive little or no independent verification.

"The Horla" begins with the narrator—a prosperous young Norman gentleman—persuading us of his happiness on a beautiful May morning. He sees a splendid Brazilian three-masted boat flow by his house, and salutes it. This gesture evidently summons the Horla, an invisible being that we later learn has been afflicting Brazil with demonic possession and subsequent madness. Horlas are evidently refined cousins of the vampires; they drink milk and water, and drain vitality from sleepers, without actually drawing blood. Whatever has been happening in Brazil, we are free to doubt precisely what is going on in Normandy. Our narrator eventually sets fire to his own house, to destroy his Horla, but neglects to tell the servants, who are consumed with their home. When the tale-teller apprehends that his Horla is still alive, he concludes by telling us that he will have to kill himself.

Clearly it is indeed *his* Horla, whether or not it made the voyage from Brazil to Normandy. The Horla is the narrator's madness, and not just the cause of his madness. Has Maupassant written the story of what it means to be possessed by syphilis? At one point the sufferer glances in the mirror and cannot see his reflection. Then he sees himself in a mist at the back of the mirror. The mist receded until sees himself completely, and of the mist of or blocking agent he cries out: "I had seen him."

The narrator says that the Horla's advent means that the reign of man is over. Magnetism, hypnotism, suggestion, are all aspects of the Horla's will. "He has come," the victim cries out, and suddenly the interloper shouts his name in one's ears: "The Horla ... he has come!"

Maupassant invents the name *Horla*; is it an ironic play upon the English word *whore*? That seems very remote, unless indeed Maupassant's venereal disease is the story's hidden center.

The horror story is a large and fascinating genre, in which Maupassant excelled, but never again as powerfully as in "The Horla." I think that it is because, on some level, he knew that he prophesied his own madness and (attempted) suicide. Maupassant is not of the artistic eminence of Turgenev, Chekhov, Henry James, or Hemingway as a short story writer, but his immense popularity is well deserved. Someone who created both "Madame Tellier's Establishment," with its amiable ecstasies, and "The Horla," with its convincing fright, was a permanent master of the story. Why read Maupassant? At his best, he will hold you as few others do. You receive pretty much what his narrative voice gives you. It is not God's plenty, but it pleases many and serves as an introduction to the more difficult pleasures of storytellers subtler than Maupassant.

Joseph Conrad

(1857–1924)

IN CONRAD'S "YOUTH" (1898), MARLOW GIVES US A BRILLIANT DESCRIPTION of the sinking of the *Judea*:

"Between the darkness of earth and heaven she was burning fiercely upon a disc of purple sea shot by the blood-red play of gleams; upon a disc of water glittering and sinister. A high, clear flame, an immense and lonely flame, ascended from the ocean, and from its summit the black smoke poured continuously at the sky. She burned furiously; mournful and imposing like a funeral pile kindled in the night, surrounded by the sea, watched over by the stars. A magnificent death had come like a grace, like a gift, like a reward to that old ship at the end of her laborious day. The surrender of her weary ghost to the keeper of the stars and sea was stirring like the sight of a glorious triumph. The masts fell just before daybreak, and for a moment there was a burst and turmoil of sparks that seemed to fill with flying fire the night patient and watchful, the vast night lying silent upon the sea. At daylight she was only a charred shell, floating still under a cloud of smoke and bearing a glowing mass of coal within.

"Then the oars were got out, and the boats forming in a line moved around her remains as if in procession—the longboat leading. As we pulled across her stern a slim dart of fire shot out viciously at us, and suddenly she went down, head first, in a great hiss of steam. The unconsumed stern was the last to sink; but the paint had gone, had cracked, had peeled off, and there were no letters, there was no word, no stubborn device that was like her soul, to flash at the rising sun her creed and her name.

The apocalyptic vividness is enhanced by the visual namelessness of the "unconsumed stern," as though the creed of Christ's people maintained both its traditional refusal to violate the Second Commandment, and its traditional affirmation of its not-to-be-named God. With the *Judea*, Conrad sinks the romance of youth's illusions, but like all losses in Conrad this submersion in the destructive element is curiously dialectical, since only experiential loss allows for the compensation of an imaginative gain in the representation of artistic truth. Originally the ephebe of Flaubert and of Flaubert's "son," Maupassant, Conrad was reborn as the narrative disciple of Henry James, the James of *The Spoils of Poynton* and *What Maisie Knew*, rather than the James of the final phase.

Ian Watt convincingly traces the genesis of Marlow to the way that "James developed the indirect narrative approach through the sensitive central intelligence of one of the characters." Marlow, whom James derided as "that preposterous magic mariner," actually represents Conrad's swerve away from the excessive strength of James's influence upon him. By always "mixing himself up with the narrative," in James's words, Marlow guarantees an enigmatic reserve that increases the distance between the impressionistic techniques of Conrad and James. Though there is little valid comparison that can be made between Conrad's greatest achievements and the hesitant, barely fictional status of Pater's *Marius the Epicurean*, Conrad's impressionism is as extreme and solipsistic as Pater's. There is a definite parallel between the fates of Sebastian Van Storck (in Pater's *Imaginary Portraits*) and Decoud in *Nostromo*.

In his 1897 "Preface" to *The Nigger of the "Narcissus,"* Conrad famously insisted that his creative task was "before all to make you *see*." He presumably was aware that he thus joined himself to a line of prose seers whose latest representatives were Carlyle, Ruskin, and Pater. There is a movement in that group from Carlyle's exuberant "Natural Supernaturalism" through Ruskin's paganization of Evangelical fervor to Pater's evasive and skeptical Epicurean materialism, with its eloquent suggestion that all we can see is the flux of sensations. Conrad exceeds Pater in the reduction of impressionism to a state of consciousness where the seeing narrator is hopelessly mixed up with the seen narrative. James may seem an impressionist when compared to Flaubert, but alongside of Conrad he is clearly shown to be a kind of Platonist, imposing forms and resolutions upon the flux of human relations by an exquisite formal geometry altogether his own.

To observe that Conrad is metaphysically less of an Idealist is hardly to argue that he is necessarily a stronger novelist than his master, James. It may suggest though that Conrad's originality is more disturbing than that of James, and may help explain why Conrad, rather than James, became the dominant influence upon the generation of American novelists that included Hemingway, Fitzgerald, and Faulkner. The cosmos of *The Sun Also Rises*, *The Great Gatsby*, and *As I Lay Dying* derives from *Heart of Darkness* and *Nostromo* rather than from *The Ambassadors* and *The Golden Bowl*. Darl Bundren is the extreme inheritor of Conrad's quest to carry impressionism into its heart of darkness in the human awareness that we are only a flux of sensations gazing outwards upon a flux of impressions.

Heart of Darkness

Heart of Darkness may always be a critical battleground between readers who regard it as an aesthetic triumph, and those like myself who doubt its ability to rescue us from its own hopeless obscurantism. That Marlow seems, at moments, not to know what he is talking about, is almost certainly one of the narrative's deliberate strengths, but if Conrad also seems finally not to know, then he necessarily loses some of his authority as a storyteller. Perhaps he loses it to death our death, or our anxiety that he will not sustain the illusion of his fiction's duration long enough for us to sublimate the frustrations it brings us.

These frustrations need not be deprecated. Conrad's diction, normally flawless, is notoriously vague throughout *Heart of Darkness*. E. M. Forster's wicked comment on Conrad's entire work is justified perhaps only when applied to *Heart of Darkness*:

> Misty in the middle as well as at the edges, the secret cask of his genius contains a vapour rather than a jewel.... No creed, in fact.

Forster's misty vapor seems to inhabit such Conradian recurrent modifiers as "monstrous," "unspeakable," "atrocious," and many more, but these are minor defects compared to the involuntary self-parody that Conrad inflicts upon himself. There are moments that sound more like James Thurber lovingly satirizing Conrad than like Conrad:

> "We had carried Kurtz into the pilot house: there was more air there. Lying on the couch, he stared through the open shutter. There was an eddy in the mass of human bodies, and the woman with helmeted head and tawny cheeks rushed out to the very brink of the stream. She put out her hands, shouted something, and all that wild mob took up the shout in a roaring chorus of articulated, rapid, breathless utterance.

"'Do you understand this?' I asked.

"He kept on looking out past me with fiery, longing eyes, with a mingled expression of wistfulness and hate. He made no answer, but I saw a smile, a smile of indefinable meaning, appear on his colorless lips that a moment after twitched convulsively. 'Do I not?' he said slowly, gasping, as if the words had been torn out of him by a supernatural power.

This cannot be defended as an instance of what Frank Kermode calls a language "needed when Marlow is not equal to the experience described." Has the experience been described here? Smiles of "indefinable meaning" are smiled once too often in a literary text if they are smiled even once. *Heart of Darkness* has taken on some of the power of myth, even if the book is limited by its involuntary obscurantism. It has haunted American literature from T.S. Eliot's poetry through our major novelists of the era 1920 to 1940, on to a line of movies that go from the *Citizen Kane* of Orson Welles (a substitute for an abandoned Welles project to film *Heart of Darkness*) on to Coppola's *Apocalypse Now*. In this instance, Conrad's formlessness seems to have worked as an aid, so diffusing his conception as to have made it available to an almost universal audience.

Anton Chekhov

(1860–1904)

Nearly a century after his death, Chekhov remains the most influential of all short story writers. There is an alternative tradition to the Chekhovian story, a rival mode invented by Kafka and developed by Borges. But such varied storytellers as James Joyce and D.H. Lawrence, Ernest Hemingway and Flannery O'Connor, essentially are part of the Chekhovian tradition (though Joyce denied it).

This brief volume examines five of Chekhov's best tales, yet I will confine this Introduction to "The Darling," Tolstoy's particular favorite. Critics have found in "The Darling" versions of the ancient Greek myths of Psyche and of Echo, and these allusions are present, but the heart of Chekhov's wonderful story is elsewhere. Tolstoy located it best when he said that the Darling, Olenka, has a soul that is "wonderful and holy." Olenka comes alive only when she lives for another, with a love so perfect that the other's concerns absorb her completely.

Though you can regard Olenka as childlike, or motherly, it seems best to follow Tolstoy, who found in her a holy soul.

Maxim Gorky memorably remarked of Chekhov that in his presence "everyone felt an unconscious desire to be simpler, more truthful, more himself," an effect that can be experienced also by Chekhov's readers. Not that the skeptical, all-knowing Chekhov is another "holy soul" in Tolstoy's sense (though Tolstoy thought so, up to a point), but undoubtedly Chekhov, like his master Shakespeare, persuades you that you can see with him what otherwise would never be apparent to you. What then can we see in "The Darling?" How should we read it, and why?

Can anyone, in reality, be so whole-hearted as Olenka? And yet, "whole-hearted" is misleading, if only because poor Olenka is reduced to an absolute emptiness when she does not have someone to love. So extreme does her condition become that it requires all of Chekhov's tact to teach us, implicitly but firmly, to avoid the vulgarity of conjectures as to her pathology. She has no opinions of her own, and yet is "a gentle, soft-hearted, compassionate girl," who lacks only a sense of self, which she can acquire only in loving. To see her as the female victim of a patriarchal society would be absurd: how would you go about raising her consciousness? There always have been and will be some like her, perhaps many, and men as well as women. Tolstoy's religious ideas were very much his own, and yet one can understand the particular sense in which this Darling or "little soul" is holy. John Keats said that he believed in nothing but the holiness of the heart's affections, and William Blake proclaimed that everything that lives is holy. Olenka is holy in that way. Keats added that he believed also in the truth of the imagination, but Olenka cannot imagine without being guided by the heart's affections.

Chekhov, like Shakespeare, solves no problems, makes no decisions for us, and quests for the total truth of the human, in the precise sense of Shakespeare's invention of the human. Olenka, though doubtless very Russian, is also universal. Chekhov's stance towards her is ironical only in a Shakespearean way: the wheel comes full circle, and we are here. Life, which has taken her three men away from Olenka, restitutes her with a foster-son, for whom she can survive. Shakespeare, as a stage dramatist, could not afford to represent banality, since even he could not hold an audience with our ordinary unhappiness. Chekhov, Shakespearean to his core, employed his stories to do what even his own plays could not do: illuminate the commonplace, without exalting or distorting it. *Three Sisters*, Chekhov's most remarkable drama, could not afford a character like Olenka, even in a minor part. It is a kind of literary miracle that Chekhov could center "The Darling" so fully upon Olenka, who can come alive only through a complete love for someone else.

O. Henry

(1862–1910)

WILLIAM SYDNEY PORTER IS A CENTRAL FIGURE IN AMERICAN POPULAR literature. He has a huge, permanent audience, and is all but identified with the short story as a genre, though he cannot be considered one of its inventors, or indeed one of its crucial innovators. His comic gifts are considerable though limited, and his careful naturalism is almost always shadowed by that of his precursor, Frank Norris. What matters most about O. Henry is the audience he has maintained for a century: ordinary readers who find themselves in his stories, not more truly and more strange, but rather as they were and are.

O. Henry's most famous tale, "The Gift of the Magi" always survives its palpable sentimentalities. The author, lovingly interested in characters founded upon his wife and himself, presents them with delicacy and compassion. Love, Dr. Samuel Johnson observed, was the wisdom of fools and the folly of the wise. That would be an admirable critical perception of Shakespeare's *King Lear* but is too grand and fierce for the gentle "Gift of the Magi" where the foolishness of love pragmatically manifests itself as a wisdom.

A more complete vision is manifested in "A Municipal Report" one of O. Henry's most complex stories: humorous, paradoxical, even a touch Borgesian in the personality of Azalea Adair, a survival of the Old South. Though the author attempts a dispassionate stance, he clearly is glad, as we are, when Azalea Adair's exploiter, the dreadful Major Wentworth Caswell, is discovered dead on a dark street:

> The gentle citizens who had known him stood about and searched their vocabularies to find some good words, if it were possible, to speak of him. One kind-looking man said, after

much thought: 'When "Cas" was about fo'teen he was one of the best spellers in school.'

"The Furnished Room" very late O. Henry, may be the darkest of all his stories. Coincidence, almost invariably overworked by the author, becomes something like a fatality here. The double suicide of lovers is made plausible by all the griminess of urban decay. A single sentence, describing a stair carpet, catches memorably the fetid atmosphere of the rooming-house, in which both lovers have died, or will die:

> It seemed to have become vegetable, to have degenerated in that rank, sunless air to lush lichen or spreading moss that grew in patches to the staircase and was viscid under the foot like organic matter.

This stands between the luxuriant rankness of Tennyson's Maud and certain Tennysonian effects in early T.S. Eliot and in Faulkner. A populist in his art, O. Henry had a repressed Symbolist poet in his spirit, and this ghostly presence helps to temper the too-evident surprises of his work.

Rudyard Kipling

(1865–1936)

TWENTY YEARS AFTER WRITING HIS ESSAY OF 1943 ON KIPLING (REPRINTED in *The Liberal Imagination*, 1951), Lionel Trilling remarked that if he could write the critique again, he would do it "less censoriously and with more affectionate admiration." Trilling, always the representative critic of his era, reflected a movement in the evaluation of Kipling that still continues in 1987. I suspect that this movement will coexist with its dialectical countermovement, of recoil against Kipling, as long as our literary tradition lasts. Kipling is an authentically *popular* writer, in every sense of the word. Stories like "The Man Who Would Be King"; children's tales from *The Jungle Books* and the *Just So Stories*; the novel *Kim*, which is clearly Kipling's masterwork; certain late stories and dozens of ballads—these survive both as high literature and as perpetual entertainment. It is as though Kipling had set out to refute the Sublime function of literature, which is to make us forsake easier pleasures for more difficult pleasures.

In his speech on "Literature," given in 1906, Kipling sketched a dark tale of the storyteller's destiny:

> There is an ancient legend which tells us that when a man first achieved a most notable deed he wished to explain to his Tribe what he had done. As soon as he began to speak, however, he was smitten with dumbness, he lacked words, and sat down. Then there arose—according to the story—a masterless man, one who had taken no part in the action of his fellow, who had no special virtues, but who was afflicted—that is the phrase—with the magic of the necessary word. He saw; he told; he described the merits of the notable deed in such a fashion, we are assured, that the words "became alive and walked up and down in the hearts of all his hearers." Thereupon, the Tribe seeing that the words were certainly

alive, and fearing lest the man with the words would hand down untrue tales about them to their children, took and killed him. But, later, they saw that the magic was in the words, not in the man.

Seven years later, in the ghastly Primal History Scene of *Totem and Taboo's* fourth chapter, Freud depicted a curiously parallel scene, where a violent primal father is murdered and devoured by his sons, who thus bring to an end the patriarchal horde. Kipling's Primal Storytelling Scene features "a masterless man" whose only virtue is "the necessary word." But he too is slain by the Tribe or primal horde, lest he transmit fictions about the Tribe to its children. Only later, in Freud, do the sons of the primal father experience remorse, and so "the dead father became stronger than the living one had been." Only later, in Kipling, does the Tribe see "that the magic was in the words, not in the man."

Freud's true subject, in his Primal History Scene, was the transference, the carrying-over from earlier to later attachments of an over-determined affect. The true subject of Kipling's Primal Storytelling Scene is not so much the Tale of the Tribe, or the magic that was in the words, but the storyteller's freedom, the masterless man's vocation that no longer leads to death, but that can lead to a death-in-life. What Kipling denies is his great fear, which is that the magic indeed is just as much in the masterless man as it is in the words.

Kipling, with his burly imperialism and his indulgences in anti-intellectualism, would seem at first out of place in the company of Walter Pater, Oscar Wilde, and William Butler Yeats. Nevertheless, Kipling writes in the rhetorical stance of an aesthete, and is very much a Paterian in the metaphysical sense. The "Conclusion" to Pater's *Renaissance* is precisely the credo of Kipling's protagonists:

> Not to discriminate every moment some passionate attitude in those about us, and in the brilliancy of their gifts some tragic dividing of forces on their ways, is, on this short day of frost and sun, to sleep before evening. With this sense of the splendour of our experience and of its awful brevity, gathering all we are into one desperate effort to see and touch, we shall hardly have time to make theories about the things we see and touch. What we have to do is to be for ever curiously testing new opinions and courting new impressions.

Frank Kermode observed that Kipling was a writer "who steadfastly preferred action and machinery to the prevalent Art for Art's Sake," but that is to misread weakly what Pater meant by ending the "Conclusion" to *The Renaissance* with what soon became a notorious formula:

We have an interval, and then our place knows us no more. Some spend this interval in listlessness, some in high passions, the wisest, at least among "the children of this world," in art and song. For our one chance lies in expanding that interval, in getting as many pulsations as possible into the given time. Great passions may give us this quickened sense of life, ecstasy and sorrow of love, the various forms of enthusiastic activity, disinterested or otherwise, which come naturally to many of us. Only be sure it is passion—that it does yield you this fruit of a quickened, multiplied consciousness. Of this wisdom, the poetic passion, the desire of beauty, the love of art for art's sake, has most; for art comes to you professing frankly to give nothing but the highest quality to your moments as they pass, and simply for those moments' sake.

Like Pater, like Nietzsche, Kipling sensed that we possess and cherish fictions because the reductive truth would destroy us. "The love of art for art's sake" simply means that we choose to believe in a fiction, while knowing that it is not true, to adopt Wallace Stevens's version of the Paterian credo. And fiction, according to Kipling, was written by daemonic forces within us, by "some tragic dividing of forces on their ways." Those forces are no more meaningful than the tales and ballads they produce. What Kipling shares finally with Pater is a deep conviction that we are caught always in a vortex of sensations, a solipsistic concourse of impressions piling upon one another, with great vividness but little consequence.

II

Kipling was a superb short story writer, who developed a defensive array of narrative devices that sometimes enhanced his fundamental vitality as an author, and at other moments perhaps impeded him. His art in later stories is extraordinarily subtle, marking his transition from the novel *Kim*, deeply influenced by Mark Twain, to oblique modes that seem to have been affected by Joseph Conrad and Henry James.

"The Man Who Would Be King" is probably Kipling's most popular story, and the public response is validly based upon the skilled, vivid characterization of the protagonists, Carnehan and Dravot. I myself find it difficult to endorse the general critical judgement that this story is an ambivalent allegory of British colonialism. Though ironical throughout, "The Man Who Would Be King" essentially is a celebration of the flamboyance and audacity of Carnehan and Dravot.

The erotic ironies of "Without Benefit of Clergy" and of "Lispeth" are tempered by what could be termed Kipling's own nostalgia for an erotic idealism that had deserted him. Ameera and Lispeth are antithetical to one another, in a contrast that depends as much upon personality as on their diverse experiences of British love. Kipling is sage enough to show us that Ameera's fulfilled nature nevertheless provokes an early death, whereas Lispeth's survival (into *Kim*) is secured by her bitterness.

Kipling's remarkable originality as storyteller triumphs in "The Church That Was At Antioch," which is composed in a marvelous prose, very much Kipling's invention:

> There filed out from behind the Little Circus four blaring trumpets, a standard, and a dozen Mounted Police. Their wise little grey Arabs sidled, passaged, shouldered, and nosed softly into the mob, as though they wanted petting, while the trumpets deafened the narrow street. An open square, near by, eased the pressure before long. Here the Patrol broke into fours, and gridironed it, saluting the images of the gods at each corner and in the centre. People stopped, as usual, to watch how cleverly the incense was cast down over the withers into the spouting cressets; children reached up to pat horses which they said they knew; family groups re-found each other in the smoky dusk; hawkers offered cooked suppers; and soon the crowd melted into the main traffic avenues.

That is a very different instrument than the prose of *Huckelberry Finn* or of the earlier Henry James. Kipling writes a middle style that *seems* timeless but of course consciously inaugurates the inception of the Twentieth century. It is an apparently plain prose that intimates a hovering darkness, as here at the close of a true shocker, "Mary Postgate":

> *But* it was a fact. A woman who had missed these things could still be useful—more useful than a man in certain respects. She thumped like a pavoir through the settling ashes at the secret thrill of it. The rain was damping the fire, but she could feel—it was too dark to see—that her work was done. There was a dull red glow at the bottom of the destructor, not enough to char the wooden lid if she slipped it half over against the driving wet. This arranged, she leaned on the poker and waited, while an increasing rapture laid hold on her. She ceased to think. She gave herself up to feel. Her long pleasure was broken by a sound that she had waited for in agony several times in her life. She leaned forward and listened, smiling. There could be no mistake. She

closed her eyes and drank it in. Once it ceased abruptly.

"Go on," she murmured, half aloud. "That isn't the end."

Then the end came very distinctly in a lull between two rain-gusts. Mary Postgate drew her breath short between her teeth and shivered from head to foot. "*That's* all right," said she contentedly, and went up to the house, where she scandalised the whole routine by taking a luxurious hot bath before tea, and came down looking, as Miss Fowler said when she saw her lying all relaxed on the other sofa, "quite handsome!"

With refined sadistic sexuality, Mary Postgate thus enjoys the slow death of a downed, badly wounded German aviator, whose agony in the shrubbery revitalizes *her*. Kipling perhaps does too much of the work for the reader, but we shudder anyway at his art. It achieves a more equivocal triumph in "Mrs. Bathurst," where we are bewildered yet suborned by indirect narrations, which come to seem more important than the dark eros that has destroyed the tale's protagonists.

When I was a child, I delighted in the *Just So Stories*, which go on sustaining me in old age. How could one improve the close of "The Cat That Walked By Himself":

Then the Man threw his two books and his little stone axe (that makes three) at the Cat, and the Cat ran out of the Cave and the Dog chased him up a tree; and from that day to this, Best Beloved, three proper Men out of five will always throw things at a Cat whenever they meet him, and all proper Dogs will chase him up a tree. But the Cat keeps his side of the bargain too. He will kill mice and he will be kind to Babies when he is in the house, just as long as they do not pull his tail too hard. But when he had done that, and between times, and when the moon gets up and night comes, he is the Cat that walks by himself, and all places are alike to him. Then he goes out to the West Wild Woods or up the Wet Wild Trees or on the Wet Wild Roofs, waving his wild tail and walking by his wild lone.

Kipling's mastery of tone and of vision is close to absolute here, and makes us realize again how many kinds of story he abounds in, and how many perspectives he creates. Of story writers in the Twentieth century, Kipling stands just below Henry James, D.H. Lawrence, and James Joyce, but he compares very adequately with Jorge Luis Borges and Isaac Babel, as the late Irving Howe justly observed.

Thomas Mann

(1875–1955)

THOMAS MANN'S GREATEST ACHIEVEMENTS WERE HIS NOVELS: *THE MAGIC Mountain*, *Joseph and his Brothers* (particularly *Tales of Jacob*) and *Doctor Faustus*. But his genius is also manifested in his novellas and stories, which demonstrate—as do the major novels—how he could transform his pervasive irony into a thousand things. Irony in Mann is not so much the condition of literary language itself as it is a composite metaphor for all of his ambivalence towards both self and society.

Death in Venice, no matter how often you reread it, brilliantly refuses to become a period piece. I suspect this is because of Mann's marvelous mask as Aschenbach, who shares both the author's covert homoeroticism and his taste for aesthetic decadence. The irony of Aschenbach's descent into death is that it is simultaneously his awakening to authentic desire.

Mario and the Magician is now perhaps something of a period piece, when Fascism has been replaced by Moslem terror as the enemy. And yet Cipolla lives: he incarnates the dangers of political charisma so permanently that the novella's permanence will return.

"Disorder and Early Sorrow" transcends its socioeconomic moment primarily because its vision of a father's love for a little daughter balances irony with an immensely subtle eros.

The novella, "Tonio Kröger," despite its ironic veneer, does seem to me to have faded. Its bourgeois nostalgias count for less now, and this once, anyway, time's revenges have overcome Mann's ironic stance.

"Felix Krull" however retains all of its ironic exuberance, as does its final expansion into Mann's playful novel of the adventures of Felix Krull, Confidence Man. The too-prevalent image of the artist-as-deceiver is subsumed by Mann's vision of the erotic intensity of the trickster's life.

Jack London

(1876–1916)

JACK LONDON DIED AT FORTY IN 1916, POSSIBLY OF A DRUG OVERDOSE. AN autodidact, the self-named Jack London worked as an oyster pirate, a seaman, a power plant laborer, but was most himself as a vagrant and a revolutionary, until he became a professional writer, and then a war correspondent. A voyager, rancher, Socialist politician, a permanent adventurer, an incessant writer: London's energies were beyond measure. He remains both a phenomenon of our imaginative literature, and a permanent figure in the American mythology.

His best stories—including "To Build a Fire," "The She-Wolf," "For the Love of a Man," "The Apostate"—surpass his novels and fantasies in literary power. The realism of the stories is so extreme and intense that they border upon hallucinatory phantasmagorias. Dogs transmute into wolves, if they are not eaten by wolves, and men struggle lest they themselves be devoured. Death is everywhere in Jack London's Klondike: freezing, starvation, wolves fuse into a composite menace.

The Call of the Wild (1903) opens with a section called "Into the Primitive," which is a fair motto for Jack London's literary quest. Here I want to center upon "The She-Wolf", the second story or episode in *White Fang* (1906). London's grim sense of determinism haunts the entire book, whose opening section "The Trail of the Meat", sums up the metaphysic of the work:

> It is not the way of the Wild to like movement. Life is an offence to it, for life is movement; and the Wild aims always to destroy movement. It freezes the water to prevent it running to the sea; it drives the sap out of the trees till they are frozen in their mighty hearts; and most ferociously and terribly of all

does the Wild harry and crush into submission man—man, who is the most restless of life, ever in revolt against the dictum that all movement must in the end come to the cessation of movement.

Jack London writes in the interval between Schopenhauer's analysis of the Will to Live and Freud's uncanny apprehension that the inanimate is our destination *and* origin, the vision of *Beyond the Pleasure Principle*. Yet London, though he gives the Wild his allegiance, retains a kind of last-ditch humanism. Bill and Henry, hunted by the wolf-pack, "two men who were not yet dead," are marked by the dignity of their mutual regard and their desperate courage. Down to three bullets and six sled-dogs, they are vastly outnumbered by the wolves. Their particular nemesis is the she-wolf, a husky sled-dog gone back to the Wild, and now a leader of the wolf-pack.

In the next episode, Bill joins the dogs as the she-wolf's victim, and Henry is a solitary survivor. It is London's peculiar power that his empathy extends equally to the she-wolf and to her human antagonists. In writers of children's literature, London's stance would be more commonplace. I cannot think of a full analogue, in adult popular literature, to London's affinity for animals except for Kipling, who so beautifully blurs the lines between children's and adult imagination. Kipling was a far more versatile and gifted writer than Jack London, and had nothing in him of London's savage primitivism. But that worship of the Wild still marks London's difference from nearly everyone else, and accounts for London's permanent appeal to readers throughout the world.

Sherwood Anderson

(1876-1941)

HISTORICALLY, SHERWOOD ANDERSON WAS A CONSIDERABLE FIGURE IN THE development of the American short story during the two decades of the 1920s and 1930s. Influenced by the naturalism of Theodore Dreiser and the prose experimentalism of Gertrude Stein, Anderson developed a narrative art sufficiently his own so that he became a crucial, early influence upon Ernest Hemingway and William Faulkner, both of whom rather ungratefully satirized him.

Anderson's obsessive "grotesques," each trapped in his or her own perspective, are generally the protagonists of his most successful stories. But my own favorite among Anderson's tales, "Death in the Woods," concerns a lifelong victim, too minimal in consciousness to be considered a grotesque. A late story, published in 1933, "Death in the Woods" tells the melancholy saga of Ma Marvin, a poor, isolated old woman who has been exploited her whole life long. Anderson neither celebrates nor laments her, but transforms her into his incantatory prose poem: "a thing so complete has its own beauty." The narrator, plainly a surrogate for Anderson, experiences both his own incarnation as an artist and his simultaneous initial sexual arousal by beholding the frozen body of the old woman, strangely white and lovely, as though she were a young girl again.

Rereading "Death in the Woods," after first confronting (and teaching) it half a century ago, I find myself both impressed and chilled by it. By centering upon the narrator's vision of Ma Marvin's death, Anderson reduces her life to its aesthetic consequences, serving as material for the story. The narrator feeds upon the old woman much as humans and animals always have fed themselves upon her. One looks for some ironic awareness of the artist's culpability in "Death in the Woods," but the irony is not there. Its absence marks both Anderson's purity as a storyteller and his limitations as well.

Stephen Crane

(1879–1900)

STEPHEN CRANE'S PRIMARY CONTRIBUTION TO AMERICAN LITERATURE remains his Civil War novel, *The Red Badge of Courage*. Yet his talents were diverse: a handful of his experimental poems continue to be vibrant, and his three finest stories are perpetually rewarding for lovers of that genre.

A war correspondent by enthusiastic profession, Stephen Crane was the Hemingway of his era, always in pursuit of material for his narrative art. "The Open Boat" is directly founded upon Crane's own experience, while "The Blue Hotel" and "The Bride Comes to Yellow Sky" reflect his travels in the American West. Crane's death, from tuberculosis at age twenty-eight, was an extraordinary loss for American letters, and his three great stories examined in this brief volume can be regarded as the most promising of his works.

"The Open Boat" intended, as Crane said, to be "after the fact," but is very different from "Stephen Crane's Own Story," his journalistic account of surviving the sinking of the *Commodore*, a cargo ship bearing arms for the Cuban rebels against Spain in January 1897. Much admired by Joseph Conrad, "The Open Boat" so handles reality as to render it phantasmagoric. The four survivors of the *Commodore* find themselves floating off a coast that absurdly declines to observe them. Even when people on shore waved to them, it is without recognition of the survivors' predicament. Compelled to make an unaided run to land, the boat is swamped in the icy water, and Crane swims ashore with the greatest difficulty. "The Open Boat" concludes with a sentence that memorializes the complex nature of the ordeal:

> When it came night, the white waves paced to and fro in the moonlight, and the wind brought the sound of the great sea's voice to the men on shore, and they felt that they could then be interpreters.

One thinks of Melville and Conrad as interpreters of the mirror of the sea; if Stephen Crane is of their visionary company, it can only be in an outsider's sense. What Crane conveys is the incomprehensibility of the sea when seen from a land-perspective. When I think of "The Open Boat," what I recall first is the frustrated helplessness of the survivors in the boat, who cannot communicate to those on shore the precariousness and desperation of shipwreck. Crane, neither a moralist like Conrad nor a Gnostic rebel like Melville, cannot quite reveal his interpretation to us.

"The Bride Comes to Yellow Sky" is a genial comedy, yet it also turns upon the absurdity of non-recognition. Scratchy Wilson, the story's insane and alcoholic gunman, cannot take in the enormous change that Jack Potter, town marshal of Yellow Sky, stands before him not only unarmed but accompanied by his new bride:

> "Well," said Wilson at last, slowly, "I s'pose it's all off now."
>
> "It's all off if you say so, Scratchy. You know I didn't make the trouble." Potter lifted his valise.
>
> "Well, I 'low it's off, Jack," said Wilson. He was looking at the ground. "Married!" He was not a student of chivalry; it was merely that in the presence of this foreign condition he was a simple child of the earlier plains. He picked up his starboard revolver, and placing both weapons in their holsters, he went away. His feet made funnel-shaped tracks in the heavy sand.

As in "The Open Boat," Crane relies upon a total clash of incongruities. Sea and land are as far apart as marriage and Scratchy Wilson, who knows only that part of his world has ended forever. Crane acts as interpreter, and yet keeps his distance from the absurd gap that is very nearly beyond interpretation.

Crane worked very hard writing "The Blue Hotel," his masterpiece of narrative. The Swede is a kind of culmination for Crane: an authentically unpleasant character, whose reality is so persuasive as to become oppressive. Lured by the myth of the West, the Swede attempts to incarnate its code, but individuates himself instead as a bully and an interloper. His fight with young Scully is a false victory, isolating him totally, until he provokes the gambler into murdering him. The rest is irony:

> The corpse of the Swede, alone in the saloon, had its eyes fixed upon a dreadful legend that dwelt a-top of the cash machine: "This registers the amount of the purchase."

Yet has the Swede purchased death or been tricked into it? Crane's final irony is to reveal that young Scully *has* been cheating at cards, thus rightly provoking the Swede to combat. Is the Easterner correct when he ends the story by asserting that five men, himself included, pragmatically murdered the Swede? I think that the reader decides differently. The Swede, and the myth of the West, are the only culprits.

James Joyce

(1882–1941)

IT IS AN ACCURATE CRITICAL COMMONPLACE TO OBSERVE THAT JOYCE'S *Dubliners* is a vision of judgment, both Dantesque and Blakean. "The Dead," masterpiece of the volume, is overtly Dantean in design, as Mary Reynolds first demonstrated. In the final cantos of the *Inferno*, we are surrounded by the frozen wastes of Cocytus, where those are buried who have betrayed country, relatives, friends, benefactors, and guests. Gabriel Conroy, protagonist of "The Dead," evidently was viewed by Joyce as such a betrayer, though in thought and emotion rather than in his actions. Joyce's implicit judgment may seem rather harsh, but then Dante was perhaps the fiercest of all poetic moralists. Gabriel Conroy is weak and parasitical, a kind of failed artist, yet most of us would not regard him as damned. But we are not Joyce, or Dante, or Blake, or Milton, and all four seers—despite their differences—would have judged many among us as being already in Hell.

Poor Gabriel has some very humane qualities, which he shares with Joyce himself, and it may be, as many critics have maintained, that the anti-hero of "The Dead" is both a Joycean self-portrait and a self-condemnation, though that is too simple to be adequate for this ambiguous and exquisite novella. I have never believed in what Sir William Empson called "the Kenner Smear," that being the Eliotic attempt by Hugh Kenner to return Joyce to the Catholic orthodoxy against which the author of *Dubliners* was in rebellion. Original depravity is no more a Joycean idea than it was Blakean. When Gabriel Conroy passes a Last Judgment upon himself, we need not agree with its severity:

> A shameful consciousness of his own person assailed him. He
> saw himself as a ludicrous figure, acting as a pennyboy for his

aunts, a nervous well-meaning sentimentalist, orating to vulgarians and idealizing his own clownish lusts, the pitiable fatuous fellow he had caught a glimpse of in the mirror.

There is something universal in that self-estimate; enough so to make many readers wince and grimace in recognition. Yet Joyce was gentler than Dante, and the creator of Poldy Bloom, the Ulysses of Dublin, was no more a dark moralist than the benign Poldy proved to be. Sublimely, Poldy was a man without hatred, curious and gentle in all things. Gabriel Conroy is no Poldy, but neither is he a resident of Dante's Inferno, whatever Joyce's symbolic design. In *Ulysses*, the symbolic and naturalistic elements in Joyce's art fuse, but in *Dubliners* they tend to pull apart. Poor Gabriel's treasons are mundane enough; they are petty, as he so frequently can be petty. Perhaps he cannot get beyond self-love, and yet the great vision that concludes "The Dead" argues for a momentary self-transcendence:

> His soul had approached that region where dwell the vast hosts of the dead. He was conscious of, but could not apprehend, their wayward and flickering existence. His own identity was fading out ...

Franz Kafka

(1883–1924)

IN HER OBITUARY FOR HER LOVER, FRANZ KAFKA, MILENA JESENSKÁ sketched a modern Gnostic, a writer whose vision was of the *kenoma*, the cosmic emptiness into which we have been thrown:

> He was a hermit, a man of insight who was frightened by life.... He saw the world as being full of invisible demons which assail and destroy defenseless man.... All his works describe the terror of mysterious misconceptions and guiltless guilt in human beings.

Milena—brilliant, fearless, and loving—may have subtly distorted Kafka's beautifully evasive slidings between normative Jewish and Jewish Gnostic stances. Max Brod, responding to Kafka's now-famous remark— "We are nihilistic thoughts that came into God's head"—explained to his friend the Gnostic notion that the Demiurge had made this world both sinful and evil. "No," Kafka replied, "I believe we are not such a radical relapse of God's, only one of His bad moods. He had a bad day." Playing straight man, the faithful Brod asked if this meant there was hope outside our cosmos. Kafka smiled, and charmingly said: "Plenty of hope—for God—no end of hope—only not for us."

Kafka, despite Gershom Scholem's authoritative attempts to claim him for Jewish Gnosticism, is both more and less than a Gnostic, as we might expect. Yahweh can be saved, and the divine degradation that is fundamental to Gnosticism is not an element in Kafka's world. But we were fashioned out of the clay during one of Yahweh's bad moods; perhaps there was divine dyspepsia, or sultry weather in the garden that Yahweh had planted in the East. Yahweh is hope, and we are hopeless. We are the jackdaws or crows, the kafkas (since that is what the name means, in Czech) whose impossibility is what the heavens signify: "The crows maintain that a single crow could destroy the heavens. Doubtless that is so, but it proves nothing against the heavens, for the heavens signify simply: the impossibility of crows."

In Gnosticism, there is an alien, wholly transcendent God, and the adept, after considerable difficulties, can find the way back to presence and fullness. Gnosticism therefore is a religion of salvation, though the most negative of all such saving visions. Kafkan spirituality offers no hope of salvation, and so is not Gnostic. But Milena Jesenská certainly was right to emphasize the Kafkan terror that is akin to Gnosticism's dread of the *kenoma*, which is the world governed by the Archons. Kafka takes the impossible step beyond Gnosticism, by denying that there is hope for us anywhere at all.

In the aphorisms that Brod rather misleadingly entitled "Reflections on Sin, Pain, Hope and The True Way," Kafka wrote: "What is laid upon us is to accomplish the negative; the positive is already given." How much Kabbalah Kafka knew is not clear. Since he wrote a new Kabbalah, the question of Jewish Gnostic sources can be set aside. Indeed, by what seems a charming oddity (but I would call it yet another instance of Blake's insistence that forms of worship are chosen from poetic tales), our understanding of Kabbalah is Kafkan anyway, since Kafka profoundly influenced Gershom Scholem, and no one will be able to get beyond Scholem's creative or strong misreading of Kabbalah for decades to come. I repeat this point to emphasize its shock value: we read Kabbalah, via Scholem, from a Kafkan perspective, even as we read human personality and its mimetic possibilities by way of Shakespeare's perspectives, since essentially Freud mediates Shakespeare for us, yet relies upon him nevertheless. A Kafkan facticity or contingency now governs our awareness of whatever in Jewish cultural tradition is other than normative.

In his diaries for 1922, Kafka meditated, on January 16, upon "something very like a breakdown," in which it was "impossible to sleep, impossible to stay awake, impossible to endure life, or, more exactly, the course of life." The vessels were breaking for him as his demoniac, writerly inner world and the outer life "split apart, and they do split apart, or at least clash in a fearful manner." Late in the evening, K. arrives at the village, which is deep in snow. The Castle is in front of him, but even the hill upon which it stands is veiled in mist and darkness, and there is not a single light visible to show that the Castle was there. K. stands a long time on a wooden bridge that leads from the main road to the village, while gazing, not at the village, but "into the illusory emptiness above him," where the Castle should be. He does not know what he will always refuse to learn, which is that the emptiness is "illusory" in every possible sense, since he does gaze at the *kenoma*, which resulted initially from the breaking of the vessels, the splitting apart of every world, inner and outer.

Writing the vision of K., Kafka counts the costs of his confirmation, in a passage prophetic of Scholem, but with a difference that Scholem sought to negate by combining Zionism and Kabbalah for himself. Kafka knew better, perhaps only for himself, but perhaps for others as well:

> Second: This pursuit, originating in the midst of men, carries one in a direction away from them. The solitude that for the most part has been forced on me, in part voluntarily sought by me—but what was this if not compulsion too?—is now losing all its ambiguity and approaches its denouement. Where is it leading? The strongest likelihood is that it may lead to madness; there is nothing more to say, the pursuit goes right through me and rends me asunder. Or I can—can I?—manage to keep my feet somewhat and be carried along in the wild pursuit. Where, then, shall I be brought? "Pursuit," indeed, is only a metaphor. I can also say, "assault on the last earthly frontier," an assault, moreover, launched from below, from mankind, and since this too is a metaphor, I can replace it by the metaphor of an assault from above, aimed at me from above.
>
> All such writing is an assault on the frontiers; if Zionism had not intervened, it might easily have developed into a new secret doctrine, a Kabbalah. There are intimations of this. Though of course it would require genius of an unimaginable kind to strike root again in the old centuries, or create the old centuries anew and not spend itself withal, but only then begin to flower forth.

Consider Kafka's three metaphors, which he so knowingly substitutes for one another. The pursuit is of ideas, in that mode of introspection which is Kafka's writing. Yet this metaphor of pursuit is also a piercing "right through me" and a breaking apart of the self. For "pursuit," Kafka then substitutes mankind's assault, from below, on the last earthly frontier. What is that frontier? It must lie between us and the heavens. Kafka, the crow or jackdaw, by writing, transgresses the frontier and implicitly maintains that he could destroy the heavens. By another substitution, the metaphor changes to "an assault from above, aimed at me from above," the aim simply being the signifying function of the heavens, which is to mean the impossibility of Kafkas or crows. The heavens assault Kafka *through his writing*; "all such writing is an assault on the frontiers," and these must now be Kafka's own frontiers. One thinks of Freud's most complex "frontier concept," more complex even than the drive: the bodily ego. The heavens assault Kafka's bodily ego, *but only through his own writing*. Certainly such an assault is not un-Jewish, and has as much to do with normative as with esoteric Jewish tradition.

Yet, according to Kafka, his own writing, were it not for the intervention of Zionism, might easily have developed into a new Kabbalah. How are we to understand that curious statement about Zionism as the blocking agent that prevents Franz Kafka from becoming another Isaac Luria? Kafka darkly and immodestly writes: "There are intimations of this." Our teacher Gershom Scholem governs our interpretation here, of necessity. Those intimations belong to Kafka alone, or perhaps to a select few in his immediate circle. They cannot be conveyed to Jewry, even to its elite, because Zionism has taken the place of messianic Kabbalah, including presumably the heretical Kabbalah of Nathan of Gaza, prophet of Sabbatai Zvi and of all his followers down to the blasphemous Jacob Frank. Kafka's influence upon Scholem is decisive here, for Kafka already has arrived at Scholem's central thesis of the link between the Kabbalah of Isaac Luria, the messianism of the Sabbatarians and Frankists, and the political Zionism that gave rebirth to Israel.

Kafka goes on, most remarkably, to disown the idea that he possesses "genius of an unimaginable kind," one that either would strike root again in archaic Judaism, presumably of the esoteric sort, or more astonishingly "create the old centuries anew," which Scholem insisted Kafka had done. But can we speak, as Scholem tried to speak, of the Kabbalah of Franz Kafka? Is there a new secret doctrine in the superb stories and the extraordinary parables and paradoxes, or did not Kafka spend his genius in the act of new creation of the old Jewish centuries? Kafka certainly would have judged himself harshly as one spent withal, rather than as a writer who "only then began to flower forth." Kafka died only two and a half years after this meditative moment, died, alas, just before his forty-first birthday. Yet as the propounder of a new Kabbalah, he had gone very probably as far as he (or anyone else) could go. No Kabbalah, be it that of Moses de Leon, Isaac Luria, Moses Cordovero, Nathan of Gaza or Gershom Scholem, is exactly easy to interpret, but Kafka's secret doctrine, if it exists at all, is designedly uninterpretable. My working principle in reading Kafka is to observe that he did everything possible to evade interpretation, which only means that what most needs and demands interpretation in Kafka's writing is its perversely deliberate evasion of interpretation. Erich Heller's formula for getting at this evasion is: "Ambiguity has never been considered an elemental force; it is precisely this in the stories of Franz Kafka." Perhaps, but evasiveness is not the same literary quality as ambiguity.

Evasiveness is purposive; it writes between the lines, to borrow a fine trope from Leo Strauss. What does it mean when a quester for a new

Negative, or perhaps rather a revisionist of an old Negative, resorts to the evasion of every possible interpretation as his central topic or theme? Kafka does not doubt guilt, but wishes to make it "possible for men to enjoy sin without guilt, almost without guilt," by reading Kafka. To enjoy sin almost without guilt is to evade interpretation, in exactly the dominant Jewish sense of interpretation. Jewish tradition, whether normative or esoteric, never teaches you to ask Nietzsche's question: "Who is the interpreter, and what power does he seek to gain over the text?" Instead, Jewish tradition asks: "Is the interpreter in the line of those who seek to build a hedge about the Torah in every age?" Kafka's power of evasiveness is not a power over his own text, and it does build a hedge about the Torah in our age. Yet no one before Kafka built up that hedge wholly out of evasiveness, not even Maimonides or Judah Halevi or even Spinoza. Subtlest and most evasive of all writers, Kafka remains the severest and most harassing of the belated sages of what will yet become the Jewish cultural tradition of the future.

II

The jackdaw or crow or Kafka is also the weird figure of the great hunter Gracchus (whose Latin name also means a crow), who is not alive but dead, yet who floats, like one living, on his death-bark forever. When the fussy Burgomaster of Riva knits his brow, asking: "And you have no part in the other world (*das Jenseits*)?", the Hunter replies, with grand defensive irony:

> I am forever on the great stair that leads up to it. On that infi-
> nitely wide and spacious stair I clamber about, sometimes up,
> sometimes down, sometimes on the right, sometimes on the
> left, always in motion. The Hunter has been turned into a but-
> terfly. Do not laugh.

Like the Burgomaster, we do not laugh. Being a single crow, Gracchus would be enough to destroy the heavens, but he will never get there. Instead, the heavens signify his impossibility, the absence of crows or hunters, and so he has been turned into another butterfly, which is all we can be, from the perspective of the heavens. And we bear no blame for that:

> "I had been glad to live and I was glad to die. Before I stepped
> aboard, I joyfully flung away my wretched load of ammunition,
> my knapsack, my hunting rifle that I had always been proud to
> carry, and I slipped into my winding sheet like a girl into her
> marriage dress. I lay and waited. Then came the mishap."

"A terrible fate," said the Burgomaster, raising his hand defensively. "And you bear no blame for it?"

"None," said the hunter. "I was a hunter; was there any sin in that? I followed my calling as a hunter in the Black Forest, where there were still wolves in those days. I lay in ambush, shot, hit my mark, flayed the skin from my victims: was there any sin in that? My labors were blessed. 'The Great Hunter of Black Forest' was the name I was given. Was there any sin in that?"

"I am not called upon to decide that," said the Burgomaster, "but to me also there seems to be no sin in such things. But then, whose is the guilt?"

"The boatman's," said the Hunter. "Nobody will read what I say here, no one will come to help me; even if all the people were commanded to help me, every door and window would remain shut, everybody would take to bed and draw the bedclothes over his head, the whole earth would become an inn for the night. And there is sense in that, for nobody knows of me, and if anyone knew he would not know where I could be found, and if he knew where I could be found, he would not know how to deal with me, he would not know how to help me. The thought of helping me is an illness that has to be cured by taking to one's bed."

How admirable Gracchus is, even when compared to the Homeric heroes! They know, or think they know, that to be alive, however miserable, is preferable to being the foremost among the dead. But Gracchus wished only to be himself, happy to be a hunter when alive, joyful to be a corpse when dead: "I slipped into my winding sheet like a girl into her marriage dress." So long as everything happened in good order, Gracchus was more than content. The guilt must be the boatman's, and may not exceed mere incompetence. Being dead and yet still articulate, Gracchus is beyond help: "The thought of helping me is an illness that has to be cured by taking to one's bed."

When he gives the striking trope of the whole earth closing down like an inn for the night, with the bedclothes drawn over everybody's head, Gracchus renders the judgment: "And there is sense in that." There is sense in that only because in Kafka's world as in Freud's, or in Scholem's, or in any world deeply informed by Jewish memory, there is necessarily sense in everything, total sense, even though Kafka refuses to aid you in getting at or close to it.

But what kind of a world is that, where there is sense in everything, where everything seems to demand interpretation? There can be sense in everything, as J.H. Van den Berg once wrote against Freud's theory of repression, only if everything is already in the past and there never again can be anything wholly new. That is certainly the world of the great normative rabbis of the second century of the Common Era, and consequently it has been the world of most Jews ever since. Torah has been given, Talmud has risen to complement and interpret it, other interpretations in the chain of tradition are freshly forged in each generation, but the limits of Creation and of Revelation are fixed in Jewish memory. There is sense in everything because all sense is present already in the Hebrew Bible, which by definition must be totally intelligible, even if its fullest intelligibility will not shine forth until the Messiah comes.

Gracchus, hunter and jackdaw, is Kafka, pursuer of ideas and jackdaw, and the endless, hopeless voyage of Gracchus is Kafka's passage, only partly through a language not his own, and largely through a life not much his own. Kafka was studying Hebrew intensively while he wrote "The Hunter Gracchus," early in 1917, and I think we may call the voyages of the dead but never-buried Gracchus a trope for Kafka's belated study of his ancestral language. He was still studying Hebrew in the spring of 1923, with his tuberculosis well advanced, and down to nearly the end he longed for Zion, dreaming of recovering his health and firmly grounding his identity by journeying to Palestine. Like Gracchus, he experienced life-in-death, though unlike Gracchus he achieved the release of total death.

"The Hunter Gracchus" as a story or extended parable is not the narrative of a Wandering Jew or Flying Dutchman, because Kafka's trope for his writing activity is not so much a wandering or even a wavering, but rather a repetition, labyrinthine and burrow-building. His writing repeats, not itself, but a Jewish esoteric interpretation of Torah that Kafka himself scarcely knows, or even needs to know. What this interpretation tells Kafka is that there is no written Torah but only an oral one. However, Kafka has no one to tell him what this Oral Torah is. He substitutes his own writing therefore for the Oral Torah not made available to him. He is precisely in the stance of the Hunter Gracchus, who concludes by saying, "'I am here, more than that I do not know, further than that I cannot go. My ship has no rudder, and it is driven by the wind that blows in the undermost regions of death.'"

III

"What is the Talmud if not a message from the distance?", Kafka wrote to Robert Klopstock, on December 19, 1932. What was all of Jewish tradition, to Kafka, except a message from an endless distance? That is surely part of the burden of the famous parable, "An Imperial Message," which concludes with you, the reader, sitting at your window when evening falls and dreaming to yourself the parable—that God, in his act of dying, has sent you an individual message. Heinz Politzer read this as a Nietzschean parable, and so fell into the trap set by the Kafkan evasiveness:

> Describing the fate of the parable in a time depleted of meta-physical truths, the imperial message has turned into the subjective fantasy of a dreamer who sits at a window with a view on a darkening world. The only real information imported by this story is the news of the Emperor's death. This news Kafka took over from Nietzsche.

No, for even though you dream the parable, the parable conveys truth. The Talmud does exist; it really is an Imperial message from the distance. The distance is too great; it cannot reach you; there is hope, but not for you. Nor is it so clear that God is dead. He is always dying, yet always whispers a message into the angel's ear. It is said to you that: "Nobody could fight his way through here even with a message from a dead man," but the Emperor actually does not die in the text of the parable.

Distance is part of Kafka's crucial notion of the Negative, which is not a Hegelian nor a Heideggerian Negative, but is very close to Freud's Negation and also to the Negative imaging carried out by Scholem's Kabbalists. But I want to postpone Kafka's Jewish version of the Negative until later. "The Hunter Gracchus" is an extraordinary text, but it is not wholly characteristic of Kafka at his strongest, at his uncanniest or most sublime.

When he is most himself, Kafka gives us a continuous inventiveness and originality that rivals Dante, and truly challenges Proust and Joyce as that of the dominant Western author of our century, setting Freud aside, since Freud ostensibly is science and not narrative or mythmaking, though if you believe that, then you can be persuaded of anything. Kafka's beast fables are rightly celebrated, but his most remarkable fabulistic being is neither animal nor human, but is little Odradek, in the curious sketch, less than a page and a half long, "The Cares of a Family Man," where the title might have been translated: "The Sorrows of a Paterfamilias." The family man narrates these five paragraphs, each a dialectical lyric in itself, beginning with one that worries the meaning of the name:

> Some say the word Odradek is of Slavonic origin, and try to account for it on that basis. Others again believe it to be of German origin, only influenced by Slavonic. The uncertainty of both interpretations allows one to assume with justice that

neither is accurate, especially as neither of them provides an intelligent meaning of the word.

This evasiveness was overcome by the scholar Wilhelm Emrich, who traced the name Odradek to the Czech word *odraditi*, meaning to dissuade anyone from doing anything. Like Edward Gorey's Doubtful Guest, Odradek is uninvited yet will not leave, since implicitly he dissuades you from doing anything about his presence, or rather something about his very uncanniness advises you to let him alone:

> No one, of course, would occupy himself with such studies if there were not a creature called Odradek. At first glance it looks like a flat star-shaped spool for thread, and indeed it does seem to have thread wound upon it; to be sure, they are only old, broken-off bits of thread, knotted and tangled together, of the most varied sorts and colors. But it is not only a spool, for a small wooden crossbar sticks out of the middle of the star, and another small rod is joined to that at a right angle. By means of this latter rod on one side and one of the points of the star on the other, the whole thing can stand upright as if on two legs.

Is Odradek a "thing," as the bemused family man begins by calling him, or is he not a childlike creature, a daemon at home in the world of children? Odradek clearly was made by an inventive and humorous child, rather in the spirit of the making of Adam out of the moistened red clay by the J writer's Yahweh. It is difficult not to read Odradek's creation as a deliberate parody when we are told that "the whole thing can stand upright as if on two legs," and again when the suggestion is ventured that Odradek, like Adam, "once had some sort of intelligible shape and is now only a broken-down remnant." If Odradek is fallen, he is still quite jaunty, and cannot be closely scrutinized, since he "is extraordinarily nimble and can never be laid hold of," like the story in which he appears. Odradek not only advises you not to do anything about him, but in some clear sense he is yet another figure by means of whom Kafka advises you against interpreting Kafka.

One of the loveliest moments in all of Kafka comes when you, the *paterfamilias*, encounter Odradek leaning directly beneath you against the banisters. Being inclined to speak to him, as you would to a child, you receive a surprise: "'Well, what's your name?' you ask him. 'Odradek,' he says. 'And where do you live?' 'No fixed abode,' he says and laughs; but it is only the kind of laughter that has no lungs behind it. It sounds rather like the rustling of fallen leaves."

"The 'I' is another," Rimbaud once wrote, adding: "So much the worse for the wood that finds it is a violin." So much the worse for the wood that finds it is Odradek. He laughs at being a vagrant, if only by the bourgeois definition of having "no fixed abode," but the laughter, not being human, is uncanny. And so he provokes the family man to an uncanny reflection, which may be a Kafkan parody of Freud's death drive beyond the pleasure principle:

> I ask myself, to no purpose, what is likely to happen to him? Can he possibly die? Anything that dies has had some kind of aim in life, some kind of activity, which has worn out; but that does not apply to Odradek. Am I to suppose, then, that he will always be rolling down the stairs, with ends of thread trailing after him, right before the feet of my children? He does no harm to anyone that I can see, but the idea that he is likely to survive me I find almost painful.

The aim of life, Freud says, is death, is the return of the organic to the inorganic, supposedly our earlier state of being. Our activity wears out, and so we die because, in an uncanny sense, we wish to die. But Odradek, harmless and charming, is a child's creation, aimless, and so not subject to the death drive. Odradek is immortal, being daemonic, and he represents also a Freudian return of the repressed, of something repressed in the *paterfamilias*, something from which the family man is in perpetual flight. Little Odradek is precisely what Freud calls a cognitive return of the repressed, while (even as) a complete affective repression is maintained. The family man introjects Odradek intellectually, but totally projects him affectively. Odradek, I now suggest, is best understood as Kafka's synecdoche for *Verneinung*; Kafka's version (not altogether un-Freudian) of Jewish Negation, a version I hope to adumbrate in what follows.

IV

Why does Kafka have so unique a spiritual authority? Perhaps the question should be rephrased. What kind of spiritual authority does Kafka have for us or why are we moved or compelled to read him as one who has such authority? Why invoke the question of authority at all? Literary authority, however we define it, has no necessary relation to spiritual authority, and to speak of a spiritual authority in Jewish writing anyway always has been to speak rather dubiously. Authority is not a Jewish concept but a Roman one, and so makes perfect contemporary sense in the context of the Roman Catholic Church, but little sense in Jewish matters, despite the squalors of Israeli politics and the flaccid pieties of American Jewish nostalgias. There is no authority without hierarchy, and hierarchy is not a very Jewish concept either. We do not want the rabbis, or anyone else, to tell us what or who is or is not Jewish. The masks of the normative conceal not only the eclecticism of Judaism and of Jewish culture, but also the nature of the J writer's Yahweh himself. It is absurd to think of Yahweh as having mere authority. He is no Roman godling who augments human activities, nor a Homeric god helping to constitute an audience for human heroism.

Yahweh is neither a founder nor an onlooker, though sometimes he can be mistaken for either or both. His essential trope is fatherhood rather than foundation, and his interventions are those of a covenanter rather than of a spectator. You cannot found an authority upon him, because his benignity is manifested not through augmentation but through creation. He does not write; he speaks, and he is heard, in time, and what he continues to create by his speaking is *olam*, time without boundaries, which is more than just an augmentation. More of anything else can come through authority, but more life is the blessing itself, and comes, beyond authority, to Abraham, to Jacob, and to David. No more than Yahweh, do any of them have mere authority. Yet Kafka certainly does have literary authority, and in a troubled way his literary authority is now spiritual also, particularly in Jewish contexts. I do not think that this is a post-Holocaust phenomenon, though Jewish Gnosticism, oxymoronic as it may or may not be, certainly seems appropriate to our time, to many among us. Literary Gnosticism does not seem to me a time-bound phenomenon, anyway. Kafka's *The Castle*, as Erich Heller has argued, is clearly more Gnostic than normative in is spiritual temper, but then so is Shakespeare's *Macbeth*, and Blake's *The Four Zoas*, and Carlyle's *Sartor Resartus*. We sense a Jewish element in Kafka's apparent Gnosticism, even if we are less prepared than Scholem was to name it as a new Kabbalah. In his 1922 Diaries, Kafka subtly insinuated that even his espousal of the Negative was dialectical:

> The Negative alone, however strong it may be, cannot suffice, as in my unhappiest moments I believe it can. For if I have gone the tiniest step upward, won any, be it the most dubious kind of security for myself, I then stretch out on my step and wait for the Negative, not to climb up to me, indeed, but to drag me down from it. Hence it is a defensive instinct in me that won't tolerate my having the slightest degree of lasting ease and smashes the marriage bed, for example, even before it has been set up.

What is the Kafkan Negative, whether in this passage or elsewhere?

Let us begin by dismissing the Gallic notion that there is anything Hegelian about it, any more than there is anything Hegelian about the Freudian *Verneinung*. Kafka's Negative, unlike Freud's, is uneasily and remotely descended from the ancient tradition of negative theology, and perhaps even from that most negative of ancient theologies, Gnosticism, and yet Kafka, despite his yearnings for transcendence, joins Freud in accepting the ultimate authority of the fact. The given suffers no destruction in Kafka or in Freud, and this given essentially is the way things are, for everyone, and for the Jews in particular. If fact is supreme, then the mediation of the Hegelian Negative becomes an absurdity, and no destructive use of such a Negative is possible, which is to say that Heidegger becomes impossible, and Derrida, who is a strong misreading of Heidegger, becomes quite unnecessary.

The Kafkan Negative most simply is his Judaism, which is to say the spiritual form of Kafka's self-conscious Jewishness, as exemplified in that extraordinary aphorism: "What is laid upon us is to accomplish the negative; the positive is already given." The positive here is the Law or normative Judaism; the negative is not so much Kafka's new Kabbalah, as it is that which is still laid upon us: the Judaism of the Negative, of the future as it is always rushing towards us.

His best biographer to date, Ernst Pawel, emphasizes Kafka's consciousness "of his identity as a Jew, not in the religious, but in the national sense." Still, Kafka was not a Zionist, and perhaps he longed not so much for Zion as for a Jewish language, be it Yiddish or Hebrew. He could not see that his astonishing stylistic purity in German was precisely his way of *not* betraying his self-identity as a Jew. In his final phase, Kafka thought of going to Jerusalem, and again intensified his study of Hebrew. Had he lived, he would probably have gone to Zion, perfected a vernacular Hebrew, and given us the bewilderment of Kafkan parables and stories in the language of the J writer and of Judah Halevi.

V

What calls out for interpretation in Kafka is his refusal to be interpreted, his evasiveness even in the realm of his own Negative. Two of his most beautifully enigmatical performances, both late, are the parable, "The Problem of Our Laws," and the story or testament "Josephine the Singer and the Mouse Folk." Each allows a cognitive return of Jewish cultural memory, while refusing the affective identification that would make either parable or tale specifically Jewish in either historical or contemporary identification. "The Problem of Our Laws" is set as a problem in the parable's first paragraph:

Our laws are not generally known; they are kept secret by the small group of nobles who rule us. We are convinced that these ancient laws are scrupulously administered; nevertheless it is an extremely painful thing to be ruled by laws that one does not know. I am not thinking of possible discrepancies that may arise in the interpretation of the laws, or of the disadvantages involved when only a few and not the whole people are allowed to have a say in their interpretation. These disadvantages are perhaps of no great importance. For the laws are very ancient; their interpretation has been the work of centuries, and has itself doubtless acquired the status of law; and though there is still a possible freedom of interpretation left, it has now become very restricted. Moreover the nobles have obviously no cause to be influenced in their interpretation by personal interests inimical to us, for the laws were made to the advantage of the nobles from the very beginning, they themselves stand above the laws, and that seems to be why the laws were entrusted exclusively into their hands. Of course, there is wisdom in that—who doubts the wisdom of the ancient laws?—but also hardship for us; probably that is unavoidable.

In Judaism, the Law is precisely what is generally known, proclaimed, and taught by the normative sages. The Kabbalah was secret doctrine, but increasingly was guarded not by the normative rabbis, but by Gnostic sectaries, Sabbatarians, and Frankists, all of them ideologically descended from Nathan of Gaza, Sabbatai Zvi's prophet. Kafka twists askew the relations between normative and esoteric Judaism, again making a synecdochal representation impossible. It is not the rabbis or normative sages who stand above the Torah but the *minim*, the heretics from Elisha ben Abuyah through to Jacob Frank, and in some sense, Gershom Scholem as well. To these Jewish Gnostics, as the parable goes on to insinuate: "The Law is whatever the nobles do." So radical a definition tells us "that the tradition is far from complete," and that a kind of messianic expectation is therefore necessary. This view, so comfortless as far as the present is concerned, is lightened only by the belief that a time will eventually come when the tradition and our research into it will jointly reach their conclusion, and as it were gain a breathing space, when everything will have become clear, the law will belong to the people, and the nobility will vanish.

If the parable at this point were to be translated into early Christian terms, then "the nobility" would be the Pharisees, and "the people" would be the Christian believers. But Kafka moves rapidly to stop such a translation: "This is not maintained in any spirit of hatred against the nobility; not at all, and by no one. We are more inclined to hate ourselves, because we have not yet shown ourselves worthy of being entrusted with the laws."

"We" here cannot be either Christians or Jews. Who then are those who "have not yet shown ourselves worthy of being entrusted with the laws"? They would appear to be the crows or jackdaws again, a Kafka or a Hunter Gracchus, wandering about in a state perhaps vulnerable to self-hatred or self-distrust, waiting for a Torah that will not be revealed. Audaciously, Kafka then concludes with overt paradox:

> Actually one can express the problem only in a sort of paradox: Any party that would repudiate not only all belief in the laws, but the nobility as well, would have the whole people behind it; yet no such party can come into existence, for nobody would dare to repudiate the nobility. We live on this razor's edge. A writer once summed the matter up in this way: The sole visible and indubitable law that is imposed upon us is the nobility, and must we ourselves deprive ourselves of that one law?

Why would no one dare to repudiate the nobility, whether we read them as normative Pharisees, Jewish Gnostic heresiarchs, or whatever? Though imposed upon us, the sages or the *minim* are the only visible evidence of law that we have. Who are we then? How is the parable's final question, whether open or rhetorical, to be answered? "Must we ourselves deprive ourselves of that one law?" Blake's answer, in *The Marriage of Heaven and Hell*, was: "One Law for the Lion and the Ox is Oppression." But what is one law for the crows? Kafka will not tell us whether it is oppression or not.

Josephine the singer also is a crow or Kafka, rather than a mouse, and the folk may be interpreted as an entire nation of jackdaws. The spirit of the Negative, dominant if uneasy in "The Problem of Our Laws," is loosed into a terrible freedom in Kafka's testamentary story. That is to say: in the parable, the laws could not be Torah, though that analogue flickered near. But in Josephine's story, the mouse folk simultaneously are *and* are not the Jewish people, and Franz Kafka both is *and* is not their curious singer. Cognitively the identifications are possible, as though returned from forgetfulness, but affectively they certainly are not, unless we can assume that crucial aspects making up the identifications have been purposefully, if other than consciously, forgotten. Josephine's piping is Kafka's story, and yet Kafka's story is hardly Josephine's piping.

Can there be a mode of negation neither conscious nor unconscious, neither Hegelian nor Freudian? Kafka's genius provides one, exposing many shades between consciousness and the work of repression, many demarcations far ghostlier than we could have imagined without him. Perhaps the ghostliest come at the end of the story:

> Josephine's road, however, must go downhill. The time will soon come when her last notes sound and die into silence. She is a small episode in the eternal history of our people, and the people will get over the loss of her. Not that it will be easy for us; how can our gatherings take place in utter silence? Still, were they not silent even when Josephine was present? Was her actual piping notably louder and more alive than the memory of it will be? Was it even in her lifetime more than a simply memory? Was it not rather because Josephine's singing was already past losing in this way that our people in their wisdom prized it so highly?
>
> So perhaps we shall not miss so very much after all, while Josephine, redeemed from the earthly sorrows which to her thinking lay in wait for all chosen spirits, will happily lose herself in the numberless throng of the heroes of our people, and soon, since we are no historians, will rise to the heights of redemption and be forgotten like all her brothers.

"I am a Memory come alive," Kafka wrote in the Diaries. Whether or not he intended it, he was Jewish memory come alive. "Was it even in her lifetime more than a simple memory?" Kafka asks, knowing that he too was past losing. The Jews are no historians, in some sense, because Jewish memory, as Yosef Yerushalmi has demonstrated, is a normative mode and not a historical one. Kafka, if he could have prayed, might have prayed to rise to the heights of redemption and be forgotten like most of his brothers and sisters. But his prayer would not have been answered. When we think of *the* Catholic writer, we think of Dante, who nevertheless had the audacity to enshrine his Beatrice in the hierarchy of Paradise. If we think of *the* Protestant writer, we think of Milton, a party or sect of one, who believed that the soul was mortal, and would be resurrected only in conjunction with the body. Think of *the* Jewish writer, and you must think of Kafka, who evaded his own audacity, and believed nothing, and trusted only in the Covenant of being a writer.

D.H. Lawrence

(1885–1930)

D.H. LAWRENCE IS NOW MOSTLY OUT OF FAVOR AND IS PARTICULARLY resented (with reason) by literary feminists. But he wrote two great novels in *The Rainbow* and *Women in Love*, and he was second only to Thomas Hardy among English poets of the Twentieth Century (setting aside the Anglo-Irish Yeats and the self-exiled-to-America Geoffrey Hill). Lawrence was also a prose-prophet and travel writer, but his most extraordinary achievement was as a tale-teller, whether in short stories like "The Prussian Officer" or in novellas like *The Man Who Died* and *The Fox*.

"The Prussian Officer" remains profoundly disturbing, and is a masterpiece of style and narration. It has particular value as a foil to *The Fox*, since the homoerotic, largely implicit drama of "The Prussian Officer" becomes almost wholly explicit in *The Fox*, a superb short novel of conflict between a man and a woman who compete for another woman.

The two girls, Banford and March, both nearing thirty, have a ambiguous relationship, evidently just short of sexual. Henry, the young soldier—nearly a decade younger than March—is a total antithesis to Banford. He is what once would have been called natural man: dignified, graceful, a born hunter, intense, instinctive. The love between March and Henry is immediate, but her history, her situation, and something recalcitrant in her nature combine to ensure that their marriage will never be complete, in his sense of a desired union of souls. Poor Banford—doomed to defeat and to a near-suicidal death—nevertheless will remain a shadow upon Henry and March. The art of *The Fox* is beautifully dispassionate: Lawrence takes no side in the contest between Banford and Henry. And yet the storyteller is not disinterested; Lawrence's stance is defined by the presence and dark fate of the fox, with whom March associates Henry. One could argue that the young man wins his wife by slaying the fox, thus displacing the imaginative hold that the creature has upon March.

Lawrence is too grand a storyteller to indulge in any obvious symbolism, and we should not translate the fox into any simplistic reduction. He is a kind of demon, in the view of the two women, since his depredations make the existence of their farm dangerously marginal. March cannot slay him, because: "She was spellbound—she knew he knew her. So he looked into her eyes, and her soul failed her. He knew her, he was not daunted." As the young soldier's forerunner, he exposes March's vulnerability to male force, her almost unconscious discontent at her situation with Banford.

March's dreams prophesy the death of Banford, and the assumption of the fox's role by Henry. Lawrence is life's partisan, but he does not devalue Banford, who is no less life than Henry is. The subtlest portrait Lawrence gives us here is that of March, rather than of Banford or Henry. March's deep force seems more passive than it is. She will not kill the fox, and she will not renounce Henry irrevocably, but something in her goes into the dream-coffin with Banford.

Katherine Anne Porter

(1890-1980)

BY THE TIME SHE WAS FIFTY, KATHERINE ANNE PORTER HAD WRITTEN AND published nearly all the fiction for which she will be remembered. Her single novel, *Ship of Fools* (1962), seemed to me an interesting failure when I first read it, more than twenty years ago, and I now find it very difficult to read through for a second time. Its critical defenders have been numerous and distinguished, including Robert Penn Warren (certainly Porter's best critic), yet it is one of those books that calls out for defense. Perhaps its author waited too long to compose *Ship of Fools*, or perhaps her genius was so admirably suited to the short novel and the short story that it was condemned to languish at greater length. What seems clear is that Porter's lasting achievement is not in *Ship of Fools*, but in "Flowering Judas," "He," "Old Mortality," "Noon Wine," "Pale Horse, Pale Rider," "The Grave" and many of their companions. She is a supreme lyricist among story writers, molding her tales with the care and delicacy that Willa Cather (whom she greatly admired) gave to such novels as *My Ántonia* and *The Lost Lady*. Like Cather, she found her truest precursor in Henry James, though her formative work seems to me rather more indebted to Joyce's *Dubliners*. But, again like Cather, her sensibility is very different from that of her male precursors, and her art, original and vital, swerves away into a rhetorical stance and moral vision peculiarly her own.

I confess to loving "Flowering Judas" most among her works, though I recognize that the aesthetic achievement of "Old Mortality," "Noon Wine" and the stories grouped as "The Old Order," is a larger one. "Still, "Flowering Judas" established Porter and rhetorically set a standard even she never surpassed. Its two most famous passages retain their aura:

A brown, shock-haired youth came and stood in her patio one

night and sang like a lost soul for two hours, but Laura could think of nothing to do about it. The moonlight spread a wash of gauzy silver over the clear spaces of the garden, and the shadows were cobalt blue. The scarlet blossoms of the Judas tree were dull purple, and the names of the colors repeated themselves automatically in her mind, while she watched not the boy, but his shadow, fallen like a dark garment across the fountain rim, trailing in the water.

... No, said Laura, not unless you take my hand, no; and she clung first to the stair rail, and then to the topmost branch of the Judas tree that bent down slowly and set her upon the earth, and then to the rocky ledge of a cliff, and then to the jagged wave of a sea that was not water but a desert of crumbling stone. Where are you taking me, she asked in wonder but without fear. To death, and it is a long way off, and we must hurry, said Eugenio. No, said Laura, not unless you take my hand. Then eat these flowers, poor prisoner, said Eugenio in a voice of pity, take and eat: and from the Judas tree he stripped the warm bleeding flowers, and held them to her lips. She saw that his hand was fleshless, a cluster of small white petrified branches, and his eye sockets were without light, but she ate the flowers greedily for they satisfied both hunger and thirst. Murderer! said Eugenio, and Cannibal! This is my body and my blood. Laura cried No! and at the sound of her own voice, she awoke trembling, and was afraid to sleep again.

The allusiveness of these passages has been analyzed as being in the mode of T.S. Eliot; indeed the allusions generally are taken to involve Eliot's "Gerontion," where "Christ the tiger" came: "In depraved May, dogwood and chestnut, flowering judas, / To be eaten, to be divided, to be drunk / Among whispers." But Porter's story, intensely erotic, is neither a "Waste Land" allegory, nor a study of Christian nostalgia. Its beautiful, sleep-walking Laura is neither a betrayer nor a failed believer, but an aesthete, a storyteller poised upon the threshold of crossing over into her own art. Porter alternatively dated "Flowering Judas" in December 1929 or January 1930. She was not much aware of Freud, then or later, but he seemed to be aware of her, so to speak, in his extraordinary essay of 1914 on narcissism, which can be read, in some places, as a portrait of Porter's Laura, the beautiful enigma of "Flowering Judas":

... there arises in the woman a certain self-sufficiency (especially when there is a ripening into beauty) which compensates her
for the social restrictions upon her object-choice. Strictly
speaking, such women love only themselves with an intensity
comparable to that of the man's love for them. Nor does their
need lie in the direction of loving, but of being loved; and that
man finds favour with them who fulfills this condition. The
importance of this type of woman for the erotic life of mankind
must be recognized as very great.

Freud goes on to observe that "one person's narcissism has a great
attraction for those others who have renounced part of their own narcissism." Laura's curious coolness, which charms us into a sense of her inac-
cessibility, is the product not of her disillusion with either the Revolution
or the Church, but of her childlike narcissism. Much of the lyrical strength
of "Flowering Judas" comes from its superb contrast between the gray-
eyed, grave Laura, who walks as beautifully as a dancer, and her obscene
serenader, the professional revolutionist Braggioni, with his tawny yellow
cat's eyes, his snarling voice, his gross intensity. Yet Braggioni is accurate
when he tells Laura: "We are more alike than you realize in some things."
Narcissist and self-loving leader of men share in a pragmatic cruelty, and
in a vanity that negates the reality of all others:

No matter what this stranger says to her, nor what her message
to him, the very cells of her flesh reject knowledge and kinship
in one monotonous word. No. No. No. She draws her strength
from this one holy talismanic word which does not suffer her
to be led into evil. Denying everything, she may walk anywhere
in safety, she looks at everything without amazement.

It is Porter's art to place Laura beyond judgment. The dream-vision
that ends the story is hardly a representation of a dream, since it is anything but a wish-fulfillment. It is the narcissist's ultimate reverie, an image
of the Judas tree representing not betrayal so much as a revelation that the
flowering Judas is oneself, one's perfect self-sufficiency. Laura, in the supposed dream or visionary projection, rightly transposes her status to that
of Eugenio, the "poor prisoner," and greedily eats the Judas flowers "for
they satisfied both hunger and thirst," as they must, being emblems of narcissistic self-passion, of the ego established by the self's investment in itself.
When Eugenio cries out: "This is my body and my blood," he is mistaken,
and we ought to give credence rather to Laura's outcry of "No!," which

wakens her from her dream. It is again the same "one holy talismanic word which does not suffer her to be led into evil," the narcissist's rejection of any love-object except herself. It is Laura's body and Laura's blood that she never ceases to absorb, and it does satisfy her hunger and her thirst.

II

Porter is a superb instance of what Frank O'Connor called *The Lonely Voice*, his title for his book on the short story, where he begins by rejecting the traditional term for the genre:

> All I can say from reading Turgenev, Chekhov, Katherine Anne Porter, and others is that the very term "short story" is a misnomer. A great story is not necessarily short at all, and the conception of the short story as a miniature art is inherently false. Basically, the difference between the short story and the novel is not one of length. It is a difference between pure and applied storytelling, and in case someone has still failed to get the point, I am not trying to decry applied storytelling. Pure storytelling is more artistic, that is all, and in storytelling I am not sure how much art is preferable to nature.

Porter too was not sure, and she deserves Robert Penn Warren's praise that hers "is a poetry that shows a deep attachment to the world's body." I add only that it shows also a deeper attachment to her own body, but I insist that is all to the good. Narcissism has gotten an absurdly bad name, but Freud certainly would snort at that, and so should we. A beautiful lyricist and a beautiful woman necessarily celebrate their own beauty, and Porter surpassingly was both. Even her stories' titles haunt me, just as photographs depicting her hold on in the memory. Warren rather surprisingly compares her to Faulkner, whose magnificence, unlike hers, generally does not come in particular phrases. I would prefer to compare her to Hart Crane, her difficult friend and impossible guest in Mexico, yet her truest contemporary, in the sense of a profound affinity in art. Porter's ambivalent account of Crane is at once a story by Porter and a visionary lyric of Hart Crane's:

> It was then that he broke into the monotonous obsessed dull obscenity which was the only language he knew after reaching a certain point of drunkenness, but this time he cursed things and elements as well as human beings. His voice at these times

... stunned the ears and shocked the nerves and caused the heart to contract. In this voice and with words so foul there is no question of repeating them, he cursed separately and by name the moon, and its light: the heliotrope, the heaven-tree, the sweet-by-night, the star jessamine, and their perfumes. He cursed the air we breathed together, the pool of water with its two small ducks huddled at the edge, and the vines on the wall and house. But those were not the things he hated. He did not even hate us, for we were nothing to him. He hated and feared himself.

This is a great poet rushing towards self-destruction, his wounded narcissism converted into aggressivity against the self, which in turn fuels the death drive, beyond the pleasure principle. Implicit in Porter's memory of Crane is the trauma of betrayed affinity, as one great lyrical artist watches another take, not her downward path to wisdom, but the way down and out to death by water. Porter, a survivor, makes the paragraph into a frighteningly effective elegy for Crane, for that supreme lyricist whose gift has become a curse, to himself and to others. Like Crane, Porter concentrated her gift, and her stories match his lyrics in their economy and in their sublime eloquence. Unlike him, she took care to survive, and perhaps we should praise her Laura, in "Flowering Judas," for the wisdom to survive, rather than condemn her for not offering herself up to be devoured by a violent though beautiful reality.

Isaac Babel

(1894–1940)

"If you need my life you may have it, but all make mistakes, God included. A terrible mistake has been made, Aunt Pesya. But wasn't it a mistake on the part of God to settle Jews in Russia, for there to be tormented worse than in Hell? How would it hurt if the Jews lived in Switzerland, where they would be surrounded by first-class lakes, mountain air, and nothing but Frenchies? All make mistakes, not God excepted."

—"How It Was Done in Odessa"

BENYA KRIK, BABEL'S OUTRAGEOUSLY INSOUCIANT GANGSTER BOSS OF Jewish Odessa, utters this defense to the bereaved Aunt Pesya, whose wretched son has just been slain by one of Benya's hoods in an exuberant error. The Jewish presence in Russia, then and now, is one of God's exuberant errors, and is both the subject and the rhetorical stance of Babel's extraordinary art as a writer of short stories. Babel's precursors were Gogol and Guy de Maupassant (and Maupassant's literary "father," Flaubert) but repeated rereadings of Babel's best stories tend to show a very different and older tradition also at work. Babel's expressionist and economical art has unmistakably Jewish literary antecedents. The late Lionel Trilling undoubtedly was the most distinguished critic to write about Babel in English, but he underestimated the Jewish element in Babel, and perhaps introduced a perspective into Babel's stories that the stories themselves repudiate.

Babel was murdered in a Stalinist purge before he was forty-seven. His work is not officially forbidden in the Soviet Union, and he was legally cleared of all charges in 1956, fifteen years after his death. Yet there are few editions of his stories, and little Soviet criticism is devoted to them. Presumably Babel's erotic intensity does not please cultural bureaucrats, and so overtly Jewish a writer, in mode and in substance, is an uncomfortable shadow in a country where teaching Hebrew is currently a legal offence. Anyone who believes that Babel's world is wholly lost ought to wander some Friday evening through "Little Odessa," as Brighton Beach in Brooklyn is called these days. Benya Krik's descendents are alive and well, a little too well, in Little Odessa. Babel is the storyteller of Jewish Odessa, the city also of Vladimir Jabotinsky, founder of the Zionist Right, teacher and inspirer of Menachem Begin and the Irgun Zvai Leumi. The Odessa of Babel was a great center of Jewish literary culture, the city also of the Hebrew poet Bialik, and of the Yiddish writer Mendele Mocher Sforim. Like Bialik and Sforim, Babel writes out of the context of Yiddish-speaking Odessa, though Babel wrote in Russian.

Trilling ought to have had second thoughts about his characterization of Babel's self-representation in *Red Cavalry* as "a Jew riding as a Cossack and trying to come to terms with the Cossack ethos." Lyutov, Babel's surrogate, is trying to survive, but hardly at the cost of coming to terms with the Cossack ethos, terms that Tolstoy in one of his modes accepted. On the contrary, Babel's Cossacks are not Tolstoyan noble savages, but are precisely the Cossacks as the Jews saw them: subhuman and bestial, mindlessly violent. Trilling imported something of his own nostalgia for the primitive into Babel, with curious results:

> Babel's view of the Cossack was more consonant with that of Tolstoy than with the traditional view of his own people. For him the Cossack was indeed the noble savage, all too savage, not often noble, yet having in his savagery some quality that might raise strange questions in a Jewish mind.

But those questions certainly are not raised in Babel's mind, the mind of the Odessa Jew, with a perpetually glowing awareness of "how it was done in Odessa." That awareness informs his two very different ways of representing violence, ways that urgently need to be contrasted when we reflect on Babel's stories. This is one way:

> Then Benya took steps. They came in the night, nine of them, bearing long poles in their hands. The poles were wrapped about with pitch-dipped tow. Nine flaming stars flared in Eichbaum's cattle yard. Benya beat the locks from the door of the cowshed and began to lead the cows out one by one. Each was received by a lad with a knife. He would overturn the cow with one blow of the fist and plunge his knife into her heart.

On the blood-flooded ground the torches bloomed like roses of fire. Shots rang out. With these shots Benya scared away the dairymaids who had come hurrying to the cowshed. After him other bandits began firing in the air. (If you don't fire in the air you may kill someone.) And now, when the sixth cow had fallen, mooing her death-moo, at the feet of the King, into the courtyard in his underclothes galloped Eichbaum."
("The King")

And meantime misfortune lurked beneath the window like a pauper at daybreak. Misfortune broke noisily into the office. And though on this occasion it bore the shape of the Jew Savka Butsis, this misfortune was as drunk as a water-carrier.

"Ho-hoo-ho," cried the Jew Savka, "forgive me, Benya, I'm late." And he started stamping his feet and waving his arms about. Then he fired, and the bullet landed in Muginstein's belly.

Are words necessary? A man was, and is no more. A harmless bachelor was living his life like a bird on a bough, and had to meet a nonsensical end. There came a Jew looking like a sailor and took a potshot not at some clay pipe or dolly but at a live man. Are words necessary?
("How It Was Done in Odessa")

This is the other way, the violence of the Cossack and not of the Odessa

But I wasn't going to shoot him. I didn't owe him a shot anyway, so I only dragged him upstairs into the parlor. There in the parlor was Nadezhda Vasilyevna clean off her head, with a drawn saber in her hand, walking about and looking at herself in the glass. And when I dragged Nikitinsky into the parlor she ran and sat down in the armchair. She had a velvet crown on trimmed with feathers. She sat in the armchair very brisk and alert and saluted me with the saber. Then I stamped on my master Nikitinsky, trampled on him for an hour or maybe more. And in that time I got to know life through and through. With shooting—I'll put it this way—with shooting you only get rid of a chap. Shooting's letting him off, and too damn easy for yourself. With shooting you'll never get at the soul, to where it is in a fellow and how it shows itself. But I don't spare myself, and I've more than once trampled an enemy for over an

hour. You see, I want to get to know what life really is, what
life's like down our way.
("The Life and Adventures of Matthew Pavlichenko")

Notices were already posted up announcing that Divisional
Commissar Vinogradov would lecture that evening on the second congress of the Comintern. Right under my window some
Cossacks were trying to shoot an old silvery-bearded Jew for
spying. The old man was uttering piercing screams and strug-
gling to get away. Then Kudrya of the machine gun section
took hold of his head and tucked it under his arm. The Jew
stopped screaming and straddled his legs. Kudrya drew out his
dagger with his right hand and carefully, without splashing
himself, cut the old man's throat. Then he knocked at the
closed window.
    "Anyone who cares may come and fetch him," he said.
"You're free to do so."
("Berestechko")

The first way is violence stylized as in a child's vision: "On the blood-
flooded ground the torches bloomed like roses of fire," and "There came a
Jew looking like a sailor and took a potshot." The second way is highly stylized also, but as in the vision of a historical Jewish irony: "With shooting
you'll never get at the soul, to where it is in a fellow and how it shows itself,"
and "carefully, without splashing himself, cut the old man's throat." When
Babel represents the violence of the Jewish gangs of the Moldavanka, he colors it as he renders Benya Krik's wardrobe: "He wore an orange suit, beneath
his cuff gleamed a bracelet set with diamonds," and "aristocrats of the
Moldavanka, they were tightly encased in raspberry waistcoats. Russet jack-
ets clasped their shoulders, and on their fleshy feet the azure leather
cracked." But Babel's representation of "the training of the famous Kniga,
the headstrong Pavlichenko, and the captivating Savitsky," is quite another
matter. The irony, ferociously subtle, is built up by nuances until the supposed nostalgia for the virtues of murderous barbarity becomes a kind of
monstrous Jewish in-joke. General Budenny's fury, when he denounced *Red
Cavalry* as a slander upon his Cossacks, was not wholly misplaced.

II

Whatever the phrase "a Jewish writer" may be taken to mean, any
meaning assigned to it that excludes Babel will not be very interesting.

Maurice Friedberg, the authority on Babel's relation to Yiddish folklore and literature, rather strangely remarks of him that: "A leftist, Russian, Jewish intellectual, particularly one strongly influenced by the adamant anti-clericalism of the French Left, could hardly be expected to return to the fold of organized religion." That Babel did not trust in the Covenant, in any strict sense, is palpably true, but the nuances of Jewish spirituality, at any time, are notoriously difficult to ascertain.

Babel's irony is so pervasive that sometimes it does threaten to turn into the irony of irony, and yet sometimes it barely masks Babel's true nostalgia, which is not exactly for the primitive. Gedali, Babel's "tiny, lonely visionary in a black top hat, carrying a big prayerbook under his arm," may be as ironic a figure as the "captivating" Savitsky, whose "long legs were like girls sheathed to the neck in shining riding boots," but the two ironies are as different as the two visions of violence, and can be conveyed again by a textual clash:

> We all of us seated ourselves side by side—possessed, liars, and idlers. In a corner, some broad-shouldered Jews who resembled fishermen and apostles were moaning over their prayerbooks. Gedali, in his green frock coat down to the ground, was dozing by the wall like a little bright bird. And suddenly I caught sight of a youth behind him, a youth with the face of Spinoza, with Spinoza's powerful brow and the wan face of a nun. He was smoking, shuddering like a recaptured prisoner brought back to his cell. The ragged Reb Mordecai crept up to him from behind, snatched the cigarette from his mouth, and ran away to me.
>
> "That's Elijah, the Rabbi's son," he declared hoarsely, bringing his bloodshot eyelids close to my face. "That's the cursed son, the last son, the unruly son."
> ("The Rabbi")

> His things were strewn about pell-mell—mandates of the propagandist and notebooks of the Jewish poet, the portraits of Lenin and Maimonides lay side by side, the knotted iron of Lenin's skull beside the dull silk of the portraits of Maimonides. A lock of woman's hair lay in a book, the Resolutions of the Party's Sixth Congress, and the margins of Communist leaflets were crowded with crooked lines of ancient Hebrew verse. They fell upon me in a mean and depressing rain—pages of the Song of Songs and revolver cartridges. The dreary rain of

sunset washed the dust in my hair, and I said to the boy who was dying on a wretched mattress in the corner:

"One Friday evening four months ago, Gedali the old-clothes-man took me to see your father, Rabbi Motale. But you didn't belong to the Party at that time, Bratslavsky."
("The Rabbi's Son")

And I don't mind telling you straight that I threw that female citizen down the railway embankment while the train was still going. But she, being big and broad, just sat there awhile, flapped her skirts, and started to go her vile way. And seeing that scatheless woman going along like that and Russia around her like I don't know what, and the peasant fields without an ear of corn and the outraged girls and the comrades lots of which go to the front but few return, I had a mind to jump out of the truck and put an end to my life or else put an end to hers. But the Cossacks took pity on me and said:

"Give it her with your rifle."

So I took my faithful rifle off the wall and washed away that stain from the face of the worker's land and the republic.
("Salt")

The pathos of Elijah the Rabbi's son is rendered bearable by a purely defensive irony, the irony of incommensurate juxtapositions, of Communist leaflets and the Hebrew Song of Songs. Irony in "Salt" dissolves all pathos, and defends Babel, not from his own affections and identifications, but from Cossack bestiality. It cannot be that Babel did not understand his own cultural affections. His first mode of irony is altogether biblical, and is neither the irony of saying one thing while meaning another, as in "Salt," nor the irony that contrasts expectation and fulfillment, for no expectations remain in "The Rabbi" and "The Rabbi's Son." Babel writes the irony of the Covenant, the incommensurateness of the Chooser and the chosen. That irony is no less Jewish than the allegory of "Salt," but its Jewishness is far more archaic.

III

The best of Babel's stories are neither in *Red Cavalry* nor in the *Tales of Odessa*, though those are my personal favorites. Babel's best work is in "The Story of My Dovecot," "First Love," "In the Basement," "Awakening," "Guy de Maupassant," "Di Grasso"—all tales of Odessa, but with the difference that they are tales of Babel himself, and not of Benya Krik. But if a single story has in it the center of Babel's achievement, it is the extraordinary, outrageous, and ultimately plangent "The End of the Old Folk's Home." Restraining himself from overtly celebrating the raffish inmates of the poorhouse by the Second Jewish Cemetery in Odessa, Babel nevertheless portrays this motley group of old men and women with a gusto and exuberance that make them the peers of Benya Krik the gangster. Gravediggers, cantors, washers of corpses, they live by their wits and unscrupulousness in hiring out their single oak coffin with a pall and silver tassels, recycling it through endless burials.

Alas, the Bolsheviks use the coffin to bury one Hersch Lugovoy with full military honors, pushing away the old men when they attempt to turn the coffin on its side so as to roll out the flag-draped corpse of the heroic and faithful Jewish Bolshevik. The rest of the story, an astonishing mixture of Dickensian pathos and Gogolian humor, portrays the doomed but still vital antics of the old folk in their final days before they are evicted from the poorhouse. With the expulsion itself, Babel achieves his finest conclusion:

> The tall horse bore him and the manager of the department of public welfare townwards. On their way they passed the old folk who had been evicted from the poorhouse. Limping, bowed beneath their bundles, they plodded along in silence. Bluff Red Army men were keeping them in line. The little carts of paralytics squeaked; the whistle of asthma, a humble gurgling issued from the breasts of retired cantors, jesters at weddings, cooks at circumcisions, and ancient shop-assistants.
>
> The sun stood high in the sky, and its rays scorched the rags trailing along the road. Their path lay along a cheerless, parched and stony highway, past huts of rammed clay, past stone-cluttered fields, past houses torn open by shells, past the Plague Mound. An unspeakably sorrowful road once led from the cemetery to Odessa.
>
> ("The End of the Old Folk's Home")

The troping of "road" for the unspeakably sorrowful procession itself is characteristic of Babel. As for the squeaking, whistling, and "humble gurgling," it is the funeral music by which Babel implicitly laments the loss of a desperate vitalism in the old folk, roisterers who in a sense are coffin-robbers, but never grave-robbers. These aged scamps are Babel's heroes and heroines, even as the Bolshevik bureaucrats and brutal Cossacks are not. Presumably Babel was another victim of Stalin's virulent anti-Semitism, but his best stories transcend his victimization. They give nothing away to the anti-Semites, nothing away even to Stalin himself. We hear in them finally a voice masterly in its ironies, yes, but also a voice of comic celebration eternally commemorating "the image of the stout and jovial Jews of the South, bubbling like cheap wine." Benya Krik's heroic funeral for the poor clerk killed by mistake is a superb exemplification of Babel's art at its most joyous:

> And the funeral was performed the next morning. Ask the cemetery beggars about that funeral. Ask the shamessim from the synagogue of the dealers in kosher poultry about it, or the old women from the Second Almshouse. Odessa had never before seen such a funeral, the world will never see such a funeral. On that day the cops wore cotton gloves. In the synagogues, decked with greenstuff and wide open, the electric lights were burning. Black plumes swayed on the white horses harnessed to the hearse. A choir of sixty headed the cortege: a choir of boys, but they sang with the voice of women. The Elders of the synagogue of the dealers in kosher poultry helped Aunt Pesya along. Behind the elders walked members of the Association of Jewish Shop Assistants, and behind the Jewish Shop Assistants walked the lawyers, doctors of medicine, and certified midwives. On one side of Aunt Pesya were the women who trade in poultry on the Old Market, and on the other side, draped in orange shawls, were the honorary dairymaids from Bugayevka. They stamped their feet like gendarmes parading on a holiday. From their wide hips wafted the odors of the sea and of milk. And behind them all plodded Ruvim Tartakovsky's employees. There were a hundred of them, or two hundred, or two thousand. They wore black frock coats with silk lapels and new shoes that squeaked like sacked suckling-pigs.
>
> ("How It Was Done in Odessa")

Those orange-shawled "honorary dairymaids," stamping their feet like gendarmes on parade while "from their wide hips wafted the odors of the sea and of milk," are Babel's true Muses. The entire paragraph becomes a phantasmagoria, a visionary evocation of a Jewish child's delight in the muscular exuberance of the Odessa mob. Babel's pragmatic sorrow was in his political context. His joy, fantastic and infectious, was in his nostalgia for his own childhood, and for the archaic and celebratory force of the Jewish tradition that claimed him, after all, for its own.

F. Scott Fitzgerald

(1896–1940)

IF ERNEST HEMINGWAY WAS THE LORD BYRON OF OUR CENTURY, SCOTT Fitzgerald is one of the prime candidates for our John Keats. Hemingway and Fitzgerald were close friends, unlike Byron and Keats, but despite the affinities between *The Sun Also Rises* and *The Great Gatsby*, the short stories by the two writers diverge greatly—in mode, stance, and style, though not always in theme. Both Hemingway and Fitzgerald stemmed in part from the novelistic procedures of Joseph Conrad, but their American precursors were very different. Hemingway acknowledged the Mark Twain of *Huckleberry Finn*, though stylistically the poetry of his prose owed much to Walt Whitman, perhaps without self-awareness. Fitzgerald turned to Henry James and Edith Wharton, whose societal contexts suited his own dreams of wealth and his Keatsian nostalgia for lost erotic possibilities.

Though *Tender Is the Night* (its title from "The Ode to a Nightingale") opens beautifully, Fitzgerald's major novel is both uneven and self-indulgent, and the unfinished *The Last Tycoon* is of mixed aesthetic quality. After *The Great Gatsby*, the best of Fitzgerald is in many of the short stories. As with Keats's odes and epic fragments, Fitzgerald's stories and novels are parables of election, of achieving or failing the severe tests of the imagination, which is seen as a power profoundly capable of destruction. "May Day" ends with Gordon Sterrett's suicide, a failed artist passing a last judgment upon himself at the age of twenty-four. A grand fantasy, "The Diamond as Big as the Ritz," achieves closure by accepting "the shabby gift of disillusion," with its protagonist urging a "divine drunkenness" upon his paramour: "let us love for a while, for a year or two, you and me." Keats's affirmation of "the holiness of the heart's affections" is not mocked, but certainly it has been distanced.

In its high artistry, "Babylon Revisited" surpasses even *The Great*

Gatsby, and compares well with Hemingway's strongest stories. Babylon is not so much Paris (in the days of Gertrude Stein and Hemingway) as it is A.E. Housman's "land of lost content." Charlie Wales, a Fitzgerald-surrogate, is more punished than his minor sins deserve. Widowed and deprived of his daughter, Wales evokes authentic pathos and suffers nostalgia and regret. A kind of elegy for the Lost Generation, "Babylon Revisited" is as adroit and balanced in style as Keats's odes and Hemingway's stories, which hover near, yet at a precise aesthetic distance.

Fitzgerald's final phase, his Hollywood years, is exemplified by "Crazy Sunday," the most finished story to emerge from those years of decline. Keats's dialectic of creation and destroying governs "Crazy Sunday," where Miles Calman pays for his art by doom-eagerness, and Joel Coles drifts towards the loss of self. The high theatricality of Stella Walker Calman is the culmination of Fitzgerald's visions of a fatal Muse, including not only Daisy in *The Great Gatsby* and Nicole in *Tender Is the Night*, but the formidable Zelda Fitzgerald herself, the last of the belles.

William Faulkner

(1897-1962)

WRITING ON FAULKNER A DOZEN YEARS AGO, I UTTERED A SECULAR prophecy that now requires adumbration:

> His grand family is Dickens run mad rather than Conrad run wild; the hideous saga of the Snopes clan, from the excessively capable Flem Snopes to the admirably named Wallstreet Panic Snopes. Flem, as David Minter observes, is refreshingly free of all influence-anxieties. He belongs in Washington D.C., and by now has reached there, and helps to staff the White House. Alas, by now he helps to staff the universities also, and soon will staff the entire nation, as his spiritual children, the Yuppies, reach middle age. Ivy League Snopes, Reagan Revolution Snopes, Jack Kemp Snopes: the possibilities are limitless. His ruined families, burdened by tradition, are Faulkner's tribute to his region. His Snopes clan is his gift to his nation.

Now, in August 1998, a Snopes is Speaker of the House, another Snopes heads the Senate, and a Snopes (of the other party) is President. Congress is about equally divided between Snopes and non-Snopes. So magnificent and comprehensive is the Vision of Snopes that it deserves to become our national political and economic mythology.

Most of the grand Snopes stories are in *The Hamlet* and *The Town*. "Barn Burning" stands quite apart, though originally Faulkner had intended it to be the very beginning of the Snopes saga. The young hero of "Barn Burning," Sarty Snopes, is a sport or changeling, wholly unlike his grim father, the horse-thief and barn-burner Abner Snopes. Whereas Ab Snopes is a kind of Satan, at war with everyone, his son Sarty manifests a finer pride, a sense of honor that triumphs over even his loyalty to the demonic Abner.

There is something sublime in the character of the boy Sartoris Snopes, a quality of a transcendental "beyond" that is not explicable either upon the basis of heredity or environment. Faulkner, despite his Gothic intensities, refused to accept any overdetermined views of human nature. "Barn Burning" is perhaps most memorable for its vivid portrait of Ab Snopes, the frightening ancestor of all the Snopes who now and permanently afflict us. But the conclusion is given wholly to young Sartoris Snopes, who will not go back to his destructive family. To the music of a whippoorwill, Sarty goes forth to a rebirth:

> He went on down the hill, toward the dark woods within which
> the liquid silver voices of the birds called unceasing—the rapid
> and urgent beating of the urgent and quiring heart of the late
> spring night. He did not look back.

Ernest Hemingway

(1899–1961)

HEMINGWAY FREELY PROCLAIMED HIS RELATIONSHIP TO *HUCKLEBERRY Finn*, and there is some basis for the assertion, except that there is little in common between the rhetorical stances of Twain and Hemingway. Kipling's *Kim*, in style and mode, is far closer to *Huckleberry Finn* than anything Hemingway wrote. The true accent of Hemingway's admirable style is to be found in an even greater and more surprising precursor:

> This grass is very dark to be from the white heads of old mothers,
> Darker than the colorless beards of old men,
> Dark to come from under the faint red roofs of mouths.

Or again:

> I clutch the rails of the fence, my gore drips, thinn'd with the
> ooze of my skin,
> I fall on the weeds and stones,
> The riders spur their unwilling horses, haul close,
> Taunt my dizzy ears and beat me violently over the head with
> whip-stocks.
> Agonies are one of my changes of garments,
> I do not ask the wounded person how he feels, I myself become
> the wounded person,
> My hurts turn livid upon me as I lean on a cane and observe.

Hemingway is scarcely unique in not acknowledging the paternity of Walt Whitman; T. S. Eliot and Wallace Stevens are far closer to Whitman than William Carlos Williams and Hart Crane were, but literary influence is a paradoxical and antithetical process, about which we continue to know all too little. The profound affinities between Hemingway, Eliot, and Stevens are not accidental, but are family resemblances due to the repressed but crucial relation each had to Whitman's work. Hemingway characteristically boasted (in a letter to Sara Murphy, February 27, 1936) that he had knocked Stevens down quite handily: "... for statistics sake Mr. Stevens is 6 feet 2 weighs 225 lbs. and ... when he hits the ground it is highly spectaculous." Since this match between the two writers took place in Key West on February 19, 1936, I am moved, as a loyal Stevensian, for statistics' sake to point out that the victorious Hemingway was born in 1899, and the defeated Stevens in 1879, so that the novelist was then going on thirty-seven, and the poet verging on fifty-seven. The two men doubtless despised one another, but in the letter celebrating his victory Hemingway calls Stevens "a damned fine poet" and Stevens always affirmed that Hemingway was essentially a poet, a judgment concurred in by Robert Penn Warren when he wrote that Hemingway "is essentially a lyric rather than a dramatic writer." Warren compared Hemingway to Wordsworth, which is feasible, but the resemblance to Whitman is far closer. Wordsworth would not have written, "I am the man, I suffer'd, I was there," but Hemingway almost persuades us he would have achieved that line had not Whitman set it down first.

II

It is now more than twenty years since Hemingway's suicide, and some aspects of his permanent canonical status seem beyond doubt. Only a few modern American novels seem certain to endure: *The Sun Also Rises*, *The Great Gatsby*, *Miss Lonelyhearts*, *The Crying of Lot 49*, and at least several by Faulkner, including *As I Lay Dying, Sanctuary, Light in August, The Sound and the Fury, Absalom, Absalom!* Two dozen stories by Hemingway could be added to the group, indeed perhaps all of *The First Forty-Nine Stories*. Faulkner is an eminence apart, but critics agree that Hemingway and Fitzgerald are his nearest rivals, largely on the strength of their shorter fiction. What seems unique is that Hemingway is the only American writer of prose fiction in this century who, as a stylist, rivals the principal poets: Stevens, Eliot, Frost, Hart Crane, aspects of Pound, W.C. Williams, Robert Penn Warren, and Elizabeth Bishop. This is hardly to say that Hemingway, at his best, fails at narrative or the representation of character. Rather, his peculiar excellence is closer to Whitman than to Twain, closer to Stevens than to Faulkner, and even closer to Eliot than to

Fitzgerald, who was his friend and rival. He is an elegiac poet who mourns the self, who celebrates the self (rather less effectively) and who suffers divisions in the self. In the broadest tradition of American literature, he stems ultimately from the Emersonian reliance on the god within, which is the line of Whitman, Thoreau, and Dickinson. He arrives late and dark in this tradition, and is one of its negative theologians, as it were, but as in Stevens the negations, the cancellings, are never final. Even the most ferocious of his stories, say "God Rest You Merry, Gentlemen" or "A Natural History of the Dead," can be said to celebrate what we might call the Real Absence. Doc Fischer, in "God Rest You Merry, Gentlemen," is a precursor of Nathanael West's Shrike in *Miss Lonelyhearts*, and his savage, implicit religiosity prophesies not only Shrike's Satanic stance but the entire demonic world of Pynchon's explicitly paranoid or Luddite visions. Perhaps there was a nostalgia for a Catholic order always abiding in Hemingway's consciousness, but the cosmos of his fiction, early and late, is American Gnostic, as it was in Melville, who first developed so strongly the negative side of the Emersonian religion of self-reliance.

III •

Hemingway notoriously and splendidly was given to overtly agonistic images whenever he described his relationship to canonical writers, including Melville, a habit of description in which he has been followed by his true ephebe, Norman Mailer. In a grand letter (September 6–7, 1949) to his publisher, Charles Scribner, he charmingly confessed, "Am a man without any ambition, except to be champion of the world, I wouldn't fight Dr. Tolstoi in a 20 round bout because I know he would knock my ears off." This modesty passed quickly, to be followed by, "If I can live to 60 I can beat him. (MAYBE)." Since the rest of the letter counts Turgenev, de Maupassant, Henry James, even Cervantes, as well as Melville and Dostoyevski, among the defeated, we can join Hemingway, himself, in admiring his extraordinary self-confidence. How justified was it, in terms of his ambitions?

It could be argued persuasively that Hemingway is the best short-story writer in the English language from Joyce's *Dubliners* until the present. The aesthetic dignity of the short story need not be questioned, and yet we seem to ask more of a canonical writer. Hemingway wrote *The Sun Also Rises* and not *Ulysses*, which is only to say that his true genius was for very short stories, and hardly at all for extended narrative. Had he been primarily a poet, his lyrical gifts would have sufficed: we do not hold it against Yeats that his poems, not his plays, are his principal glory. Alas, neither Turgenev nor Henry James, neither Melville nor Mark Twain provide true agonists for Hemingway. Instead, de Maupassant is the apter rival. Of Hemingway's intensity of style in the briefer compass, there is no question, but even *The Sun Also Rises* reads now as a series of epiphanies, of brilliant and memorable vignettes.

Much that has been harshly criticized in Hemingway, particularly in *For Whom the Bell Tolls*, results from his difficulty in adjusting his gifts to the demands of the novel. Robert Penn Warren suggests that Hemingway is successful when his "system of ironies and understatements is coherent." When incoherent, then, Hemingway's rhetoric fails as persuasion, which is to say, we read *To Have and Have Not or For Whom the Bell Tolls* and we are all too aware that the system of tropes is primarily what we are offered. Warren believes this not to be true of *A Farewell to Arms*, yet even the celebrated close of the novel seems now a worn understatement:

> But after I had got them out and shut the door and turned off the light it wasn't any good. It was like saying good-by to a statue. After a while I went out and left the hospital and walked back to the hotel in the rain.·

Contrast this to the close of "Old Man at the Bridge," a story only two and a half pages long:

> There was nothing to do about him. It was Easter Sunday and the Fascists were advancing toward the Ebro. It was a gray overcast day with a low ceiling so their planes were not up. That and the fact that cats know how to look after themselves was all the good luck that old man would ever have.

The understatement continues to persuade here because the stoicism remains coherent, and is admirably fitted by the rhetoric. A very short story concludes itself by permanently troping the mood of a particular moment in history. *Vignette* is Hemingway's natural mode, or call it hard-edged vignette: a literary sketch that somehow seems to be the beginning or end of something longer, yet truly is complete in itself. Hemingway's style encloses what ought to be unenclosed, so that the genre remains subtle yet trades its charm for punch. But a novel of three hundred and forty pages (*A Farewell to Arms*) which I have just finished reading again (after twenty years away from it) cannot sustain itself upon the rhetoric of vignette. After many understatements, too many, the reader begins to believe that he is reading a Hemingway imitator, like the accomplished

John O'Hara, rather than the master himself. Hemingway's notorious fault is the monotony of repetition, which becomes a dulling litany in a somewhat less accomplished imitator like Nelson Algren, and sometimes seems self-parody when we must confront it in Hemingway.

Nothing is got for nothing, and a great style generates defenses in us, particularly when it sets the style of an age, as the Byronic Hemingway did. As with Byron, the color and variety of the artist's life becomes something of a veil between the work and our aesthetic apprehension of it. Hemingway's career included four marriages (and three divorces); service as an ambulance driver for the Italians in World War I (with an honorable wound); activity as a war correspondent in the Greek-Turkish War (1922), the Spanish Civil War (1937–39), the Chinese-Japanese War (1941) and the War against Hitler in Europe (1944–45). Add big-game hunting and fishing, safaris, expatriation in France and Cuba, bullfighting, the Nobel prize, and ultimate suicide in Idaho, and you have an absurdly implausible life, apparently lived in imitation of Hemingway's own fiction. The final effect of the work and the life together is not less than mythological, as it was with Byron and with Whitman and with Oscar Wilde. Hemingway now is myth, and so is permanent as an image of American heroism, or perhaps more ruefully the American illusion of heroism. The best of Hemingway's work, the stories and *The Sun Also Rises*, are also a permanent part of the American mythology. Faulkner, Stevens, Frost, perhaps Eliot, and Hart Crane were stronger writers than Hemingway, but he alone in this American century has achieved the enduring status of myth.

Jorge Luis Borges

(1899–1986)

FOR THE GNOSTIC IN BORGES, AS FOR THE HERESIARCH IN HIS MYTHIC Uqbar, "mirrors and fatherhood are abominable because they multiply and disseminate that universe," the visible but illusory labyrinth of men. Gnostics rightly feel at ease with Jung, and very unhappy with Freud, as Borges does, and no one need be surprised when the ordinarily gentlemanly and subtle Argentine dismisses Freud "either as a charlatan or as a madman," for whom "it all boils down to a few rather unpleasant facts." Masters of the tale and the parable ought to avoid the tape-recorder, but as Borges succumbed, an admirer may be grateful for the gleaning of a few connections between images.

The gnostic gazes into the mirror of the fallen world and sees, not himself, but his dark double, the shadowy haunter of his phantasmagoria. Since the ambivalent God of the gnostics balances good and evil in himself, the writer dominated by agnostic vision is morally ambivalent also. Borges is imaginatively a gnostic, but intellectually a skeptical and naturalistic humanist. This division, which has impeded his art, making of him a far lesser figure than gnostic writers like Yeats and Kafka, nevertheless has made him also an admirably firm moralist, as these taped conversations show.

Borges has written largely in the spirit of Emerson's remark that the hint of the dialectic is more valuable than the dialectic itself. My own favorite among his tales, the cabbalistic "Death and the Compass," traces the destruction of the Dupin-like Erik Lönnrot, whose "reckless discernment" draws him into the labyrinthine trap set by Red Scharlach the Dandy, a gangster worthy to consort with Babel's Benya Krik. The greatness of Borges is in the aesthetic dignity both of Lönnrot, who at the point of death criticizes the labyrinth of his entrapment as having redundant lines, and of Scharlach, who just before firing promises the detective a better labyrinth, when he hunts him in some other incarnation.

The critics of the admirable Borges do him violence by hunting him as Lönnrot pursued Scharlach, with a compass, but he has obliged us to choose his own images for analysis. Freud tells us that: "In a psychoanalysis the physician always gives his patient (sometimes to a greater and sometimes to a lesser extent) the conscious anticipatory image by the help of which he is put in a position to recognise and to grasp the unconscious material." We are to remember that Freud speaks of therapy, and of the work of altering ourselves, so that the analogue we may find between the images of physician and romancer must be an imperfect one. The skillful analyst moreover, on Freud's example, gives us a single image, and Borges gives his reader a myriad; but only mirror, labyrinth, compass will be gazed at here.

Borges remarks of the first story he wrote, "Pierre Menard, Author of the Quixote," that it gives a sensation of tiredness and skepticism, of "coming at the end of a very long literary period." It is revelatory that this was his first tale, exposing his weariness of the living labyrinth of fiction even as he ventured into it. Borges is a great theorist of poetic influence; he has taught us to read Browning as a precursor of Kafka, and in the spirit of this teaching we may see Borges himself as another Childe Roland coming to the Dark Tower, while consciously not desiring to accomplish the Quest. Are we also condemned to see him finally more as a critic of romance than as a romancer? When we read Borges—whether his essays, poems, parables, or tales—do we not read glosses upon romance, and particularly on the skeptic's self-protection against the enchantments of romance?

Borges thinks he has invented one new subject for a poem—in his poem "Limits"—the subject being the sense of doing something for the last time, seeing something for the last time. It is extraordinary that so deeply read a man-of-letters should think this, since most strong poets who live to be quite old have written on just this subject, though often with displacement or concealment. But it is profoundly self-revelatory that a theorist of poetic influence should come to think of this subject as his own invention, for Borges has been always the celebrator of things-in-their-farewell, always a poet of loss. Though he has comforted himself, and his readers, with the wisdom that we can lose only what we never had, he has suffered the discomfort also of knowing that we come to recognize only what we have encountered before, and that all recognition is self-recognition. All loss is of ourselves, and even the loss of falling-out of love is, as Borges would say, the pain of returning to others, not to the self. Is this the wisdom of romance, or of another mode entirely?

What Borges lacks, despite the illusive cunning of his labyrinths, is precisely the extravagance of the romancer; he does not trust his own vagrant impulses. He sees himself as a modestly apt self-marshaller, but he is another Oedipal self-destroyer. His addiction to the self-protective economy and overt knowingness of his art is his own variety of the Oedipal anxiety, and the pattern of his tales betrays throughout an implicit dread of family-romance. The gnostic mirror of nature reflects for him only Lönnrot's labyrinth "of a single line which is invisible and unceasing," the line of all those enchanted mean streets that fade into the horizon of the Buenos Aires of his phantasmagoria. The reckless discerner who is held by the symmetries of his own mythic compass has never been reckless enough to lose himself in a story, to our loss, if not to his. His extravagance, if it still comes, will be a fictive movement away from the theme of recognition, even against that theme, and towards a larger art. His favorite story, he says, is Hawthorne's "Wakefield," which he describes as being "about the man who stays away from home all those years."

John Steinbeck

(1902–1968)

EUDORA WELTY, WRITING ABOUT THE SHORT STORIES OF D.H. LAWRENCE, memorably caught the essential strangeness of Lawrence's art of representation.

> For the truth seems to be that Lawrence's characters don't really speak their words—not conversationally, not to one another—they are *not* speaking on the street, but are playing like fountains or radiating like the moon or storming like the sea, or their silence is the silence of wicked rocks. It is borne home to us that Lawrence is writing of our human relationships on earth in terms of eternity, and these terms set Lawrence's form. The author himself appears in authorship in places like the moon, and sometimes smiles on us while we stand there under him.

Welty was a short story writer almost of Lawrence's eminence; John Steinbeck was not. But Steinbeck's stories owed as much to Lawrence as Steinbeck's novels did to Hemingway. Though he resented Hemingway, Steinbeck wrote a softened version of Hemingway's famous style. Lawrence affected Steinbeck very differently; something in Steinbeck implicitly understood that his own naturalistic reductionism limited his art. D.H. Lawrence's heroic vitalism, his ability to endow his character with qualities "playing like fountains," appealed to Steinbeck's repressed transcendentalism. The best of Steinbeck's stories are in Lawrence's mode, and not Hemingway's.

"The Chrysanthemums," which seems to me the most interesting of Steinbeck's stories, is far closer to Lawrence's intense evocations of the soul than it is to the version of Darwinism that Steinbeck had taken over from the marine biologist, Edward Ricketts. Several critics have noted how close Steinbeck's Elisa Allen is to Lawrence's March in *The Fox*, except that Elisa is a balked figure from the beginning. Her repressed sexuality, aroused by the encounter with the wandering tinker, is not likely to be gratified by her inadequate husband, or indeed by any other man. In Lawrence, Elisa would become a lover of women, but Steinbeck evades such an intimation, though the imaginative logic of his story probably argues for such a future.

How much change takes place in Elisa between the start and the conclusion of the story? When we first see her, she is all potential, a force not yet exercised although she is in the middle of the journey.

> She was cutting down the old year's chrysanthemum stalks with a pair of short and powerful scissors. She looked down toward the men by the tractor shed now and then. Her face was eager and mature and handsome; even her work with the scissors was over-eager, over-powerful. The chrysanthemum stems seemed too small and easy for her energy.

At the story's close, she is crying weakly, "as if she were an old woman." We need to know more if we are to understand whether this is only a momentary defeat or the reassertion of a pattern. In Lawrence or in Welty we *would* know, because both of them were able to write "of our human relationships on earth in terms of eternity." Steinbeck as a writer never could achieve that, not even in *The Grapes of Wrath*. "The Chrysanthemums" shows Steinbeck bruising himself against his own imaginative limitations, unable to bruise himself an exit from himself. The *materia poetica* for a larger and more intense art is there in the story, but Steinbeck could not realize it.

Eudora Welty

(1909-2001)

EUDORA WELTY DIVIDES HER REMARKABLE BRIEF AUTOBIOGRAPHY, *ONE Writer's Beginnings*, into three parts: "Listening," "Learning to See," "Finding A Voice." Gentle yet admonitory, these titles instruct us in how to read her stories and novels, a reading that necessarily involves further growth in our sense of inwardness. Certain of her stories never cease their process of journeying deep into interior regions we generally reserve only for personal and experiential memories. Doubtless they differ from reader to reader; for me they include "A Still Moment" and "The Burning."

Mark Twain has had so varied a progeny among American writers that we hardly feel surprise when we reflect that Welty and Hemingway both emerge from *Huckleberry Finn*. All that Welty and Hemingway share as storytellers is Twain's example. Their obsessive American concern is Huck's: the freedom of a solitary joy, intimately allied to a superstitious fear of solitude. Welty's people, like Hemingway's, and like the self-representations of our major poets—Whitman, Dickinson, Stevens, Frost, Eliot, Hart Crane, R.P. Warren, Roethke, Elizabeth Bishop, Ashbery, Merrill, and Ammons—all secretly believe themselves to be no part of the creation and all feel free only when they are quite alone.

In *One Writer's Beginning:*, Welty comments upon "A Still Moment":

> "A Still Moment"—another early story—was a fantasy, in which the separate interior visions guiding three highly individual and widely differing men marvelously meet and converge upon the same single exterior object. All my characters were actual persons who had lived at the same time, who would have been strangers to one another, but whose lives had actually taken them at some point to the same neighborhood. The scene was

in the Mississippi wilderness in the historic year 1811—"*anno mirabilis*," the year the stars fell on Alabama and lemmings, or squirrels perhaps, rushed straight down the continent and plunged into the Gulf of Mexico, and an earthquake made the Mississippi River run backwards and New Madrid, Missouri, tumbled in and disappeared. My real characters were Lorenzo Dow the New England evangelist, Murrell the outlaw bandit and murderer on the Natchez Trace, and Audubon the painter; and the exterior object on which they all at the same moment set their eyes is a small heron, feeding.

Welty's choices—Lorenzo Dow, James Murrell, Audubon—are all obsessed solitaries. Dow, the circuit rider, presumably ought to be the least solipsistic of the three, yet his fierce cry as he rides on at top speed—"I must have souls! And souls I must have!"—is evidence of an emptiness that never can be filled:

It was the hour of sunset. All the souls that he had saved and all those he had not took dusky shapes in the mist that hung between the high banks, and seemed by their great number and density to block his way, and showed no signs of melting or changing back into mist, so that he feared his passage was to be difficult forever. The poor souls that were not saved were darker and more pitiful than those that were, and still there was not any of the radiance he would have hoped to see in such a congregation.

As Dow himself observes, his eyes are in a "failing proportion to my loving heart always," which makes us doubt his heart. He loves his wife, Peggy, effortlessly since she is in Massachusetts and he is galloping along on the Old Natchez Trace. Indeed, their love can be altogether effortless, consisting as it does of a marriage proposal, accepted as his first words to her, a few hours of union, and his rapid departure south for evangelical purposes, pursued by her first letter declaring that she, like her husband, fears only death, but never mere separation.

This remarkable hunter of souls, intrepid at evading rapacious Indians or Irish Catholics, can be regarded as a sublime lunatic, or merely as a pure product of America:

Soon night would descend, and a camp-meeting ground ahead would fill with its sinners like the sky with its stars. How he hungered for them! He looked in prescience with a longing of love over the throng that waited while the flames of the torches threw change, change, change over their faces. How could he bring them enough, if it were not divine love and sufficient warning of all that could threaten them? He rode on faster. He was a filler of appointments, and he filled more and more, until his journeys up and down creation were nothing but a shuttle, driving back and forth upon the rich expanse of his vision. He was homeless by his own choice, he must be everywhere at some time, and somewhere soon. There hastening in the wilderness on his flying horse he gave the night's torch-lit crowd a premature benediction, he could not wait. He spread his arms out, one at a time for safety, and he wished, when they would all be gathered in by his tin horn blasts and the inspired words would go out over their heads, to brood above the entire and passionate life of the wide world, to become its rightful part.

He peered ahead. "Inhabitants of Time! The wilderness is your souls on earth!" he shouted ahead into the treetops. "Look about you, if you would view the conditions of your spirit, put here by the good Lord to show you and afright you. These wild places and these trails of awesome loneliness lie nowhere, nowhere, but in your heart."

Dow is his own congregation, and his heart indeed contains the wild places and awesomely lonesome trails through which he endlessly rushes. His antithesis is provided by the murderous James Murrell, who suddenly rides at Dow's side, without bothering to look at him. If Dow is a mad angel, Murrell is a scarcely sane devil, talking to slow the evangelist down, without realizing that the sublimely crazy Lorenzo listens only to the voice of God:

Murrell riding along with his victim-to-be, Murrell, riding, was Murrell talking. He told away at his long tales, with always a distance and a long length of time flowing through them, and all centered about a silent man. In each the silent man would have done a piece of evil, a robbery or a murder, in a place of long ago, and it was all made for the revelation in the end that the silent man was Murrell himself, and the long story had happened yesterday, and the place *here*—the Natchez Trace. It would only take one dawning look for the victim to see that all of this was another story and he himself had listened his way into it, and that he too was about to recede in time (to where the dread was forgotten) for some listener and to live for a listener in the long ago. Destroy the present!—that must have been the first thing that was whispered in Murrell's heart—the living moment and the man that lives in it must die before you can go on. It was his habit to bring the journey—which might even take days—to a close with a kind of ceremony. Turning his face at last into the face of the victim, for he had never seen him before now, he would tower up with the sudden height of a man no longer the tale teller but the speechless protagonist, silent at last, one degree nearer the hero. Then he would murder the man.

Since Murrell is capable of observing nothing whatsoever, he does not know what the reader knows, which is that Lorenzo is not a potential victim for this self-dramatizing Satanist. Whatever the confrontation between angel and devil might have brought (and one's surmise is that Murrell might not have survived), the crucial moment is disturbed by the arrival of a third, the even weirder Audubon:

> Audubon said nothing because he had gone without speaking a word for days. He did not regard his thoughts for the birds and animals as susceptible, in their first change, to words. His long playing on the flute was not in its origin a talking to himself. Rather than speak to order or describe, he would always draw a deer with a stroke across it to communicate his need of venison to an Indian. He had only found words when he discovered that there is much otherwise lost that can be noted down each item in its own day, and he wrote often now in a journal, not wanting anything to be lost the way it had been, all the past, and he would write about a day, "Only sorry that the Sun Sets."

These three extraordinarily diverse obsessives share a still moment, in which "a solitary snowy heron flew down not far away and began to feed beside the marsh water." To Lorenzo, the heron's epiphany is God's love become visible. To Murrell, it is "only whiteness ensconced in darkness," a prophecy of the slave, brigand, and outcast rebellion he hopes to lead in the Natchez country. To Audubon it is precisely what it is, a white heron he must slay if he is to be able to paint, a model that must die in order to become a model. Welty gives us no preference among these three:

What each of them had wanted was simply *all*. To save all souls, to destroy all men, to see and record all life that filled this world—all, all—but now a single frail yearning seemed to go out of the three of them for a moment and to stretch toward this one snowy, shy bird in the marshes. It was as if three whirlwinds had drawn together at some center, to find there feeding in peace a snowy heron. Its own slow spiral of flight could take it away in its own time, but for a little it held them still, it laid quiet over them, and they stood for a moment unburdened....

To quest for *all* is to know anything but peace, and "a still moment" is only shared by these three questers in a phantasmagoria. When the moment ends with Audubon's killing of the bird, only Lorenzo's horrified reaction is of deep import or interest. Murrell is content to lie back in ambush and await travelers more innocent, who will suit his Satanic destiny as Lorenzo and Audubon could not. Audubon is also content to go on, to fulfill his vast design. But Lorenzo's epiphany has turned into a negative moment and though he will go on to gather in the multitudes, he has been darkened:

In the woods that echoed yet in his ears, Lorenzo riding slowly looked back. The hair rose on his head and his hands began to shake with cold, and suddenly it seemed to him that God Himself, just now, thought of the Idea of Separateness. For surely He had never thought of it before, when the little white heron was flying down to feed. He could understand God's giving Separateness first and then giving Love to follow and heal in its wonder; but God had reversed this, and given Love first and then Separateness, as though it did not matter to Him which came first. Perhaps it was that God never counted the moments of Time; Lorenzo did that, among his tasks of love. Time did not occur to God. Therefore—did He even know of it? How to explain Time and Separateness back to God, Who had never thought of them, Who could let the whole world come to grief in a scattering moment?

This is a meditation on the verge of heresy, presumably Gnostic, rather than on the border of unbelief. Robert Penn Warren, in a classical early essay on "Love and Separateness in Eudora Welty" (1944), reads the dialectic of Love and Separateness here as the perhaps Blakean contraries of Innocence and Experience. On this reading, Welty is an ironist of limits and of contamination, for whom knowledge destroys love, almost as though love could survive only upon enchanted ground. That may underestimate both Lorenzo and Welty. Pragmatically, Lorenzo has been unchanged by the still moment of love and its shattering into separateness; indeed he is as unchanged as Murrell or Audubon. But only Lorenzo remains haunted by a vision, by a particular beauty greater than he can account for, and yet never can deny. He will change some day, though Welty does not pursue that change.

II

The truth of Welty's fictive cosmos, for all her preternatural gentleness, is that love always does come first, and always does yield to an irreparable separateness. Like her true mentor, Twain, she triumphs in comedy because her deepest awareness is of a nihilistic "unground" beyond consciousness or metaphysics, and comedy is the only graceful defense against that cosmological emptiness. Unlike Faulkner and Flannery O'Connor, she is, by design, a genial writer, but the design is a subtler version of Twain's more urgent desperation. "A Still Moment," despite its implications, remains a fantasy of the continuities of quest. Rather than discuss one of her many masterpieces of humorous storytelling, I choose instead "The Burning," which flamboyantly displays her gift for a certain grim sublimity, and which represents her upon her heights, as a stylist and narrator who can rival Hemingway in representing the discontinuities of war and disaster.

"The Burning" belongs to the dark genre of Southern Gothic, akin to Faulkner's "A Rose for Emily" and O'Connor's "A Good Man Is Hard to Find." Welty, as historical a storyteller as Robert Penn Warren, imagines an incident from Sherman's destructive march through Georgia. The imagining is almost irrealistic in its complexity of tone and indirect representation, so that "The Burning" is perhaps the most formidable of all Welty's stories, with the kind of rhetorical and allusive difficulties we expect to encounter more frequently in modern poetry than in modern short stories. Writing on form in D.H. Lawrence's stories, Welty remarked on "the unmitigated shapelessness of Lawrence's narrative" and sharply noted that his characters would only appear deranged if they began to speak on the streets as they do in the stories:

> For the truth seems to be that Lawrence's characters don't really speak their words—not conversationally, not to one another—they are not speaking on the street, but are playing like fountains or radiating like the moon or storming like the sea,

or their silence is the silence of wicked rocks. It is borne home to us that Lawrence is writing of our human relationships on earth in terms of eternity, and these terms set Lawrence's form. The author himself appears in authorship in places like the moon, and sometimes smites us while we stand there under him.

The characters of Welty's "The Burning" fit her description of Lawrence's men and women; their silence too is the silence of wicked rocks. Essentially they are only three: two mad sisters, Miss Theo and Miss Myra, and their slave, called Florabel in the story's first published version (*Harper's Bazaar*, March, 1951). The two demented high-born ladies are very different; Miss Theo is deep-voiced and domineering, Miss Myra gentler and dependent. But little of the story is seen through their eyes or refracted through either's consciousness. Florabel, an immensely passive being, sees and reacts, in a mode not summarized until nearly the end of the story, in its first printed form:

Florabel, with no last name, was a slave. By the time of that moment on the hill, her kind had been slaves in a dozen countries and that of their origin for thousands of years. She let everything be itself according to its nature—the animate, the inanimate, the symbol. She did not move to alter any of it, not unless she was told to and shown how. And so she saw what happened, the creation and the destruction. She waited on either one and served it, not expecting anything of it but what she got; only sooner or later she would seek protection somewhere. Herself was an unknown, like a queen, somebody she had heard called, even cried for. As a slave she was earth's most detached visitor. The world had not touched her—only possessed and hurt her, like a man; taken away from her, like a man; turned another way from her and left her, like a man. Her vision was clear. She saw what was there and had not sought it, did not seek it yet. (It was *her* eyes that were in the back of her head, her vision that met itself coming the long way back, unimpeded, like the light of stars.) The command to loot was one more fading memory. Many commands had been given her, some even held over from before she was born; delayed and miscarried and interrupted, they could yet be fulfilled, though it was safer for one once a slave to hear things a second time, a third, fourth, hundredth, thousandth, if they were to be carried out to the letter. In that noon quiet after conflict there might have been only the two triumphant, the mirror which was a symbol in the world and Florabel who was standing there; it was the rest that had died of it.

The mirror, "a symbol in the world," is in this first version of "The Burning" a synecdoche for the fragmented vision of both mad sisters and their slave. In rewriting the story, Welty uses the mirror more subtly. Delilah (as Florabel is now named) sees Sherman's soldiers and their apocalyptic white horse directly as they enter the house, and she runs to tell Miss Theo and Miss Myra. They deign to look up and observe the intruders in the mirror over the fireplace. Throughout the rest of the catastrophic narrative, the sisters behold everything that transpires as though in a mirror. Clearly they have spent their lives estranging reality as though looking in a mirror, and they move to their self-destruction as though they saw themselves only as images. The violence that prepares for the burning is thus rendered as phantasmagoria:

> The sisters showed no surprise to see soldiers and Negroes alike (old Ophelia in the way, talking, talking) strike into and out of the doors of the house, the front now the same as the back, to carry off beds, tables, candlesticks, washstands, cedar buckets, china pitchers, with their backs bent double; or the horses ready to go; or the food of the kitchen bolted down— and so much of it thrown away, this must be a second dinner; or the unsilenceable dogs, the old pack mixed with the strangers and fighting with all their hearts over bones. The last skinny sacks were thrown on the wagons—the last flour, the last scraping and clearing from Ophelia's shelves, even her pepper-grinder. The silver Delilah could count was counted on strange blankets and then, knocking against the teapot, rolled together, tied up like a bag of bones. A drummer boy with his drum around his neck caught both Miss Theo's peacocks, Marco and Polo, and wrung their necks in the yard. Nobody could look at those bird-corpses; nobody did.

The strangling of the peacocks is a presage of the weirdest sequence in "The Burning," in which Miss Theo and Miss Myra hang themselves from a tree, with Delilah assisting as ordered. It is only when the sisters are dead that we begin to understand that "The Burning" is more Delilah's story than it ever could have been theirs. A baby, Phinny, who had been allowed to perish in the fire (Welty does not allow us to know why), turns out to have been begotten by Miss Theo's and Miss Myra's brother Benton upon Delilah:

> The mirror's cloudy bottom sent up minnows of light to the brim where now a face pure as a water-lily shadow was floating. Almost too small and deep down to see, they were quivering, leaping to life, fighting, aping old things Delilah had seen done in this world already, sometimes what men had done to Miss Theo and Miss Myra and the peacocks and to slaves, and sometimes what a slave had done and what anybody now could do to anybody. Under the flicker of the sun's licks, then under its whole blow and blare, like an unheard scream, like an act of mercy gone, as the wall-less light and July blaze struck through from the opened sky, the mirror felled her flat.
>
> She put her arms over her head and waited, for they would all be coming again, gathering under her and above her, bees saddled like horses out of the air, butterflies harnessed to one another, bats with masks on, birds together, all with their weapons bared. She listened for the blows, and dreaded that whole army of wings—of flies, birds, serpents, their glowing enemy faces and bright kings' dresses, that banner of colors forked out, all this world that was flying, striking, stricken, falling, gilded or blackened, mortally splitting and falling apart, proud turbans unwinding, turning like the spotted dying leaves of fall, spiraling down to bottomless ash; she dreaded the fury of all the butterflies and dragonflies in the world riding, blades unconcealed and at point—descending, and rising again from the waters below, down under, one whale made of his own grave, opening his mouth to swallow Jonah one more time.
>
> Jonah!—a homely face to her, that could still look back from the red lane he'd gone down, even if it was too late to speak. He was her Jonah, her Phinny, her black monkey; she worshiped him still, though it was long ago he was taken from her the first time.

Delilah, hysterical with fear, shock, and anguish, has fallen into the mirror world of the mad sisters, her self-slain mistresses. She is restored to some sense of reality by her search for Phinny's bones. Carrying them, and what she can save of the sisters' finery, she marches on to what is presented ambiguously either as her own freedom, or her death, or perhaps both together:

Following the smell of horses and fire, to men, she kept in the wheel tracks till they broke down at the river. In the shade underneath the burned and fallen bridge she sat on a stump and chewed for a while, without dreams, the comb of a dirtdauber. Then once more kneeling, she took a drink from the Big Black, and pulled the shoes off her feet and waded in.

Submerged to the waist, to the breast, stretching her throat like a sunflower stalk above the river's opaque skin, she kept on, her treasure stacked on the roof of her head, hands laced upon it. She had forgotten how or when she knew, and she did not know what day this was, but she knew—it would not rain, the river would not rise, until Saturday.

This extraordinary prose rises to an American sublime that is neither grotesque nor ironic. Welty, in her *On Short Stories*, asked the question: "Where does beauty come from, in the short story?" and answered only that beauty was a result:

It *comes*. We are lucky when beauty comes, for often we try and it should come, it could, we think, but then when the virtues of our story are counted, beauty is standing behind the door.

I do not propose to count the virtues of "The Burning," or even of "A Still Moment." Both narratives are as thoroughly written through, fully composed, as the best poems of Wallace Stevens or of Hart Crane, or the strongest of Hemingway's stories, or Faulkner's *As I Lay Dying*. American writing in the twentieth century touches the sublime mode only in scattered instances, and always by reaching the frontier where the phantasmagoric, and the realism of violence, are separated only by ghostlier demarcations, keener sounds. Welty's high distinction is that in her the demarcations are as ghostly, the sounds as keen, as they are in her greatest narrative contemporaries, Faulkner and Hemingway.

John Cheever

(1912-1982)

I JOIN THE MANY READERS UNABLE TO ABANDON A PERPETUAL RETURN TO John Cheever's "The Country Husband" (1955). One cannot quite name Cheever as one of the modern American story-writers of the highest eminence: Hemingway, Faulkner, Willa Cather, Katherine Anne Porter, Scott Fitzgerald, Eudora Welty, Flannery O'Connor. Still, Cheever compares favorably enough with the second order: Sherwood Anderson, Nabokov, Malamud, Updike, Ozick, Ann Beattie, Carver, the Canadian Alice Munro. Like them, he lacks the enduring originality of Hemingway and Faulkner, but Cheever is as assured and finished as Nabokov or Updike.

"The Country Husband" disturbs me intensely with each rereading, even if it is less universal a vision of failed marriage than clearly it intends to be. Francis Weed is no Everyman, even though I have encountered (and taught) many of his potential doubles. Aesthetically, Cheever's story gains more than it loses by a certain forlorn inner solitude in Weed, who sometimes suggests a misplaced writer, like Cheever himself.

Where does one locate the haunting splendor of "The Country Husband"? Not, I think, in the idea of order that will keep the Weeds together until death, dubious as their love is for one another. Francis Weed's authentic desire hardly is for the babysitter, but for the image in his memory of the Norman young woman, shorn and stripped as punishment, with "some invaluable grandeur in her nakedness." A superb artist, John Cheever lacquers his surfaces, but the dark power of his best stories' undersong is their reliance upon the deviance of the sexual drive into sadomasochism.

Julio Cortázar

(1914–1984)

"BESTIARY" IS A PERMANENT SHORT STORY NOT SO MUCH BECAUSE OF ITS fantastic tiger, but through its subtle and nuanced presentation of Isabel's passion for Rema, a passion that turns murderous and destroys her sadistic uncle, by means of the tiger.

I don't see any allegory in the tiger, though one cannot say that sometimes a tiger is only a tiger. But "Bestiary" is something of a jest, as well as the account of Isabel's desire for Rema's soft touch. The long, stunning final paragraph of the story, rendered here with great skill by Paul Blackburn, haunts me frequently:

> The Kid was eating already, the newspaper beside him, there was hardly enough room for Isabel to rest her arm. Luis was the last to come from his room, contented as he always was at noon. They ate, Nino was talking about the snails, the snail eggs in the reeds, the collection itself, the sizes and the colors. He was going to kill them by himself, it hurt Isabel to do it, they'd put them to dry on a zinc sheet. After the coffee came and Luis looked at them with the usual question. Isabel got up first to look for don Roberto, even though don Roberto had already told her before. She made the round of the porch and when she came in again, Rema and Nino had their heads together over the snail box, it was like a family photograph, only Luis looked up at her and she said, "It's in the Kid's study," and stayed watching how the Kid shrugged his shoulders, annoyed, and Rema who touched a snail with a fingertip, so delicately that her finger even seemed part snail. Afterwards, Rema got up to go look for more sugar, and Isabel tailed along behind her babbling

until they came back in laughing from a joke they'd shared in the pantry. When Luis said he had no tobacco and ordered Nino to look in his study, Isabel challenged him that she'd find the cigarettes first and they went out together. Nino won, they came back in running and pushing, they almost bumped into the Kid going to the library to read his newspaper, complaining because he couldn't use his study. Isabel came over to look at the snails, and Luis waiting for her to light his cigarette as always saw that she was lost, studying the snails which were beginning to ooze out slowly and move about, looking at Rema suddenly, but dropping her like a flash, captivated by the snails, so much so that she didn't move at the Kid's first scream, they were all running and she was still standing over the snails as if she did not hear the Kid's new choked cry. Luis beating against the library door, don Roberto coming in with the dogs, the Kid's moans amid the furious barking of the dogs, and Luis saying over and over again, "But it was in his study! She said it was in his own study!", bent over the snails willowy as fingers, like Rema's fingers maybe, or it was Rema's hand on her shoulder, made her raise her head to look at her, to stand looking at her for an eternity, broken by her ferocious sob into Rema's skirt, her unsettled happiness, and Rema running her hand over her hair, quieting her with a soft squeeze of her fingers and a murmuring against her ear, a stuttering as of gratitude, as of an unnamable acquiescence.

The rhetorical effect here party depends upon *montage*. Isabel scarcely can rest either her arm or her desire for Rema, because of the aggressive presence of the Kid, her threatening uncle. When Isabel and Rema return together from the pantry, have they shared more than a joke? The superb final sentence is an ecstasy of sexual happiness, in which Rema accepts gratefully Isabel's gift of destroying the Kid, and silently assents to the assassination. There is something almost infinitely suggestive of a potential, mutual bliss awaiting Rema and Isabel in Cortázar's final cadences.

Shirley Jackson

(1919-1965)

ONLY A FEW MONTHS BEFORE I WROTE THIS INTRODUCTION, THE TALIBAN in Kabul, Afghanistan, stoned to death a woman caught in adultery. As Islamic fundamentalists, the Taliban follow their interpretation of the Koran, itself based upon Jewish-Christian sources.

Shirley Jackson's famous story "The Lottery" is peculiarly horrifying because it is so artfully affectless. In what seems an upper New England setting, an annual ritual takes place. We are in a village so small that everyone appears to know everyone else, and the stoning to death of Mrs. Hutchinson has no relation to morality or to explicit religion. Perhaps that adds to the shock effect of "The Lottery," a story that depends upon tapping into a universal fear of arbitrary condemnation, and of sanctioned violence.

Like so many of Shirley Jackson's stories, "The Lottery" makes me brood upon the element of tendentiousness that renders her so problematic in aesthetic terms. Jackson always had too palpable a design upon her readers; her effects are as calculated as Poe's. Poe alas is inescapable: his nightmares were and are universal. This salvages him, despite the viciousness of his prose style, and absence of nuance in his work. Since he is greatly improved by translation (even into English), Poe has endured, and cannot be discarded, or even evaded.

"The Lottery," like most of Jackson's stories, is crisply written and cunningly plotted. But it scarcely bears rereading, which is (I think) the test for canonical literature. Jackson knows too well exactly what she is doing, and on rereading, so do we. You *can* learn certain rudiments of narration from "The Lottery," and yet the story's strict economy, which is its overt strength, is finally something of a stunt. It is as though we are at a magic show and we can see all the wires that ought to be invisible.

Literary judgment depends upon comparison, and so it is valid to contrast "The Lottery" to other stories that frighten us by relying upon archaic rituals. There is a long American tradition of Gothic narrative, whose masters include Hawthorne, Faulkner, and Flannery O'Connor. But these are masters and disturb us more profoundly than Jackson can, because they portray the complexities of character and personality without which we cannot permanently be moved. As fabulists, the masters of American Gothic carry us on a journey to the interior. Jackson certainly aspired to be more than an entertainer; her concern with sorceries, ancient and modern, was authentic and even pragmatic. But her art of narration stayed on the surface, and could not depict individual identities. Even "The Lottery" wounds you once, and once only.

J.D. Salinger

(1919–)

J.D. Salinger's principal achievement is *The Catcher in the Rye* (1951), a short novel that has attained a kind of mythological status in the nearly half-century since its publication. His short stories, in book form, constitute three equally slender volumes: *Nine Stories* (1953), *Franny and Zooey* (1961), and *Raise High the Roof Beam, Carpenters and Seymour: An Introduction* (1963). Salinger has been silent for the last 35 years, a silence that seems only to have enhanced his popularity. Fresh generations of the young continue to find something of themselves in his work.

Rereading Salinger's 13 principal stories, after a third of a century, is a mixed experience, at least for me. All of them have their period-piece aspect, portraits of a lost New York City, or of New Yorkers elsewhere, in the post-World War II America that vanished forever in the "cultural revolution" (to call it that) of the late 1960s. Holden Caulfield and the Glass siblings charm me now-though sometimes they make me wince—because they are so archaic. Their humane spirituality, free of dogma and of spite, has to be refreshing as we drift toward the millennium.

Of the six stories to which this volume is devoted, "Raise High the Roof Beam, Carpenters" now reads best, not for its "religious pluralism" (as one critic characterized it) but simply for high good humor. Its representation of being stuck in a Manhattan traffic jam has an exuberance that Salinger rarely manifests either in his persons or his plots. Zaniness rather than Zen-Taoist pluralism saves the story from Salinger's inverted sentimentalities and from Glass sibling affections, too frequently emotions in excess of their objects. Salinger's ear for dialogue, inherited from Hemingway and Fitzgerald, is acutely manifested throughout a bizarre narrative in which little happens, which is to be preferred to Seymour's suicide in "A Perfect Day for Bananafish," or Franny's fainting fit in the story that bears her name.

Salinger's stylistic skills are beyond question; his stories perform precisely as he intends. And they hold up as storytelling, even if their social attitudes and spiritual stances frequently now seem archaic or quaint. Their problem is that the Glass siblings are not exactly memorable as individuals. Even poor Seymour is more a type than a vivid consciousness in himself. "Seymour: an Introduction" I find impossible to reread, partly because his brother Buddy, the narrator, never knows when to stop, and again who can tolerate this kind of smug spirituality?

Seymour once said that all we do our whole lives is go from one little piece of Holy Ground to the next. Is he never wrong?

A reader might well retort: when is Seymour right? The accuracy of Seymour's mystic insight is not the issue. Stories must have narrative values, or they cease to be stories, and "Seymour: an Introduction" fails to be a story. That may be why Salinger's fiction stopped. Contemplation can be a very valuable mode of being and existence, but it has no stories to tell.

Italo Calvino

(1923–1985)

Invisible Cities

THE ERA OF OUR CONTEMPORARY MODES OF LITERARY CRITICISM WILL PASS; perhaps already it has passed. Fictions that accommodate themselves too readily in regard to our modes will pass with them. Nabokov, Borges, García Márquez, John Barth may seem less available to generations later than our own. Much of Italo Calvino doubtless will dwindle away also, but not *Invisible Cities*, though aspects of the book might almost be judged as having been written for sensibilities schooled by semiotics and by reader-response criticism. But those aspects are not central to *Invisible Cities*, and this work's outer armature will not engage me here. Like much of Kafka, *Invisible Cities* will survive its admirers' modes of apprehension, because it returns us to the pure form of romance, genre of the marvelous, realm of speculation. With Kafka's *The Great Wall of China*, it renews a literature we require yet can no longer deserve or earn.

Like Kublai Khan, we do not necessarily believe everything that Marco Polo describes, but we too suffer the emptiness of the evening land and hope to discern the tracery of some pattern that will compensate us for our endless errors about life. Doubtless, as Nietzsche remarked, errors about life are necessary for life, and doubtless also, as Emerson said, we demand victory, a victory to the senses as well as to the soul. But error and triumph alike induce emptiness, the cosmological emptiness that Gnosticism named as the *kenoma*, the waste land or waste wilderness of all literary romance. Calvino's Kublai Khan is a Demiurge inhabiting that, *kenoma*, "an endless formless ruin," in which we know that "corruption's gangrene has spread too far to be healed by our scepter, that the triumph over enemy sovereigns has made us the heirs of their long undoing."

The Invisible Cities dot the *kenoma*, but are no part of it, being sparks of the original Abyss, our foremother and forefather, and so the source of everything still that is best and oldest in us. It is not in the *kenoma* that "the foreigner hesitating between two women always encounters a third" or where you find "bergamot, sturgeon roe, astrolabes, amethysts." As sparks of the true *pneuma* or breath-soul, the Invisible Cities are not psyches or personalities, despite their names. They do not represent women but rather forewomen, as it were, for in truth all of them are at once memories, desires, and signs, that is, repressions and the return of the repressed. Perhaps it is Calvino's peculiar genius (though he shares it with Kafka) that we scarcely can distinguish, in his pages, the repressed and its return, as here in the city called Anastasia:

> At the end of three days, moving southward, you come upon Anastasia, a city with concentric canals watering it and kites flying over it. I should now list the wares that can profitably be bought here: agate, onyx, chrysoprase, and other varieties of chalcedony; I should praise the flesh of the golden pheasant cooked here over fires of seasoned cherry wood and sprinkled with much sweet marjoram; and tell of the women I have seen bathing in the pool of a garden and who sometimes—it is said—invite the stranger to disrobe with them and chase them in the water. But with all this, I would not be telling you the city's true essence; for while the description of Anastasia awakens desires one at a time only to force you to stifle them, when you are in the heart of Anastasia one morning your desires waken all at once and surround you. The city appears to you as a whole where no desire is lost and of which you are a part, and since it enjoys everything you do not enjoy, you can do nothing but inhabit this desire and be content. Such is the power, sometimes called malignant, sometimes benign, that Anastasia, the treacherous city, possesses; if for eight hours a day you work as a cutter of agate, onyx, chrysoprase, your labor which gives form to desire takes from desire its form, and you believe you are enjoying Anastasia wholly when you are only its slave.

That antithetical will, seen by Nietzsche as art's willed revenge against time, triumphs here even as it does in Yeats or Kafka. The Great Khan, Kublai, learns from Marco that his empire is nothing but a summa of emblems, a zodiac of phantasmagorias. Learning all the emblems will give Kublai no sense of possession, for on the day of total knowledge, the

Khan will be an emblem among emblems, at once again the sign of repression and of return from such defense. Marco's use, both for himself and for Kublai, is to teach what he uniquely learns: that the meaning of any Invisible City can only be another Invisible City, not itself:

> And Marco's answer was: "Elsewhere is a negative mirror. The traveler recognizes the little bit that is his, discovering the much he has not had and will never have.

As Marco's narration proceeds, the Invisible Cities accomplish the paradox of growing ever more fantastic, yet ever more pragmatic. Calvino remembers implicitly Nietzsche's dark aphorism: we only find words to describe what we now feel contempt towards, however dearly we once held it in our hearts. The Khan reminds Marco that he never mentions Venice, and the traveler reveals the secret of every quester for the Alien God, for the City forever lost:

> "Memory's images, once they are fixed in words, are erased," Polo said, "Perhaps I am afraid of losing Venice all at once, if I speak of it. Or perhaps, speaking of other cities, I have already lost it, little by little."

It is fitting that Calvino's last Invisible City should be his most imaginative, or perhaps it is merely that he has described my own dream, the extraordinary Berenice, at once the unjust city, and the city of the just. Berenice is a nightmare of repetitions, in which the just and the unjust constantly undergo metamorphoses into one another:

> From these data it is possible to deduce an image of the future Berenice, which will bring you closer to knowing the truth than any other information about the city as it is seen today. You must nevertheless bear in mind what I am about to say to you: in the seed of the city of the just, a malignant seed is hidden, in its turn: the certainty and pride of being in the right—and of being more just than many others who call themselves more just than the just. This seed ferments in bitterness, rivalry, resentment; and the natural desire of revenge on the unjust is colored by a yearning to be in their place and to act as they do. Another unjust city, though different from the first, is digging out its space within the double sheath of the unjust and just Berenices.
> Having said this, I do not wish your eyes to catch a distorted

image, so I must draw your attention to an intrinsic quality of this unjust city germinating secretly inside the secret just city: and this is the possible awakening—as if in an excited opening of windows—of a later love for justice, not yet subjected to rules, capable of reassembling a city still more just than it was before it became the vessel of injustice. But if you peer deeper into this new germ of justice you can discern a tiny spot that is spreading like the mounting tendency to impose what is just through what is unjust, and perhaps this is the germ of an immense metropolis....

From my words you will have reached the conclusion that the real Berenice is a temporal succession of different cities, alternately just and unjust. But what I wanted to warn you about is something else: all the future Berenices are already present in this instant, wrapped one within the other, confined, crammed, inextricable.

This is not merely a parable about the relativity of justice, or the selfish virtue of self-righteousness, but a vision of the ambivalence of all Eros, since the just Berenice is an Eros, and the unjust a Thanatos. Just and unjust, Berenice is the city of jealousy, of natural possessiveness, of the malignant seed hidden in the heart of Eros. The shadow of our mortality, cast upwards by the earth into the heavens, stopped at the sphere of Venus, as Shelley liked to remind us, but in Berenice the shadow never stops. A temporal succession of love and death, just and unjust, is real enough, and dark enough. But Calvino gives us a stronger warning: every instant holds all the future Berenices, inextricably crammed together, death drive and libido confined in one chiasmus, wrapped one within the other. Fortunately, *Invisible Cities* ends more amiably, when Marco insists that the inferno need not be the last landing place, if only we: "seek and learn to recognize who and what, in the midst of the inferno, are not inferno, then make them endure, give them space." Dante would have dismissed this with grim irony, but we cannot afford to do so.

As coda, I resort to an extraordinary short story, "The Night Driver," in Calvino's *t zero*. The narrator, in a telephone argument with Y, his mistress, tells her he wishes to end their affair. Y replies that she will phone Z, the narrator's rival. To save the affair, the narrator undertakes a night drive on the superhighway that connects his city to that of his beloved. In rain and darkness, at high speed, the narrator does not know if Z is outspeeding him towards Y, or if Y herself perhaps started towards his city, with motives akin to his own. In a mad parody of semiotics, the narrator, Y, and Z have become signs or signals or messages, weird reductions in a system:

Naturally, if I were absolutely alone on this superhighway, if I saw no other cars speeding in either direction, then everything would be much clearer, I would be certain that Z hasn't moved to supplant me, nor has Y moved to make peace with me, facts I might register as positive or negative in my accounting, but which would in any case leave no room for doubt. And yet if I had the power of exchanging my present state of uncertainty for such a negative certainty, I would refuse the bargain without hesitation. The ideal condition for excluding every doubt would prevail if in this part of the world there existed only three automobiles: mine, Y's, and Z's; then no other car could proceed in my direction except Z's, and the only car heading in the opposite direction would surely be Y's. Instead, among the hundreds of cars that the night and the rain reduce to anonymous glimmers, only a motionless observer situated in a favorable position could distinguish one car from the other and perhaps recognize who is inside. This is the contradiction in which I find myself: if I want to receive a message I must give up being a message myself, but the message I want to receive from Y— namely, that Y has made herself into a message—has value only if I in turn am a message, and on the other hand the message I am has meaning only if Y doesn't limit herself to receiving it like any ordinary receiver of messages but if she also is that message I am waiting to receive from her.

By now to arrive in B, go up to Y's house, find that she has remained there with her headache brooding over the causes of our quarrel, would give me no satisfaction; if then Z were to arrive also a scene would be the result, histrionic and loathsome; and if instead I were to find out that Z has prudently stayed home or that Y didn't carry out her threat to telephone him, I would feel I had played the fool. On the other hand, if I had remained in A, and Y had gone there to apologize to me, I would have seen Y through different eyes, a weak woman, clinging to me, and something between us would have changed. I can no longer accept any situation other than this transformation of ourselves into the messages of ourselves. And what about Z? Even Z must not escape our fate, he too must be transformed into the message of himself; it would be terrible if I were to run to Y jealous of Z and if Y were running to me, repentant, avoiding Z, while actually Z hasn't remotely thought of stirring from his house.

To be made into a message, or to give up such a making, alike are catastrophe creations. Calvino's sublimely funny summary seems to me his finest sentence ever: "I can no longer accept any situation other than the transformation of ourselves into the messages of ourselves." But are we not then back in the City of Berenice? Y, Z, and the narrator are all residents of that Invisible City, where the just and the unjust twine into one another, love cannot be distinguished from jealousy, and repression scarcely can be told from what returns from it. Night drivers go between Invisible Cities, transforming memory and desire into homogenous signs, confounding eyes and names, contaminating the sky with the dead. The alternative to such night driving indeed is to "seek and learn to recognize who and what, in the midst of the inferno, are not inferno, then make them endure, give them space."

Nonexistent Knight

I devote my remarks here to my other favorite in Calvino, the delightful *Nonexistent Knight*. Calvino's triumph in this exquisite and zany fantasy is that Agilulf, who is only an empty suit of white shining armor, nevertheless endears himself to the delighted reader. The book's glory is the development of Agilulf from a martinet of exemplary will power to a charmingly devoted quester heroically seeking to restore the authenticity of his knighthood. When poor Agilulf despairs, and abandons his armor as a legacy to Raimbaud, he vanishes forever, and we are saddened.

An absurd yet heartening atmosphere of good will pervades *The Nonexistent Knight*. All its characters, the Saracens included, have verve and style. Calvino even is able to invest Charlemagne with a sly sense of humor. The spirit of Ariosto, Calvino's true precursor, hovers nearly, and informs the personalities of Bradamante/Theodora and Raimbaud, and of Sophronia and Torrismund.

Entirely Calvino's own are the nonexistent knight Sir Agilulf and his squire, the uncanny clown Gurduloo, who cannot hold on to the consciousness that *he* truly has a body. In a superb contrast, Calvino metaphysically exploits the difference between knight and squire, and the normative Raimbaud.

> As Agilulf dragged a corpse along he thought, 'Oh corpse, you have what I never had or will have: a carcass. Or rather you *have*; you *are* this carcass, that which at times, in moments of despondency, I find myself envying in men who exist. Fine! I can truly call myself privileged, I who can live without it and do all; all, of course, which seems most important to me; many

things I manage to do better than those who exist, since I lack their usual defects of coarseness, carelessness, incoherence, smell. It's true that someone who exists always has a particular attitude of his own to things, which I never manage to have. But if their secret is merely here, in this bag of guts, then I can do without it. This valley of disintegrating naked corpses disgusts me no more than does the flesh of living human beings.'

As Gurduloo dragged a corpse along he thought, 'Corpsy, your farts stink even more than mine. I don't know why everyone mourns you so. What's it you lack? Before you used to move, now your movement is passed on to the worms you nourish. Once you grew nails and hair; now you'll ooze slime which will make grass in the field grow higher towards the sun. You will became grass, then milk for cows which will eat the grass, blood of the baby that drinks their milk, and so on. Don't you see you get more out of life than I do, corpsy?'

As Raimbaud dragged a dead man along he thought, 'Oh corpse, I have come rushing here only to be dragged along by the heels like you. What is this frenzy that drives me, this mania for battle and for love, when seen from the place where your staring eyes gaze and your flung-back head knocks over stones? It's that I think of, oh corpse, it's that you make me think of: but does anything change? Nothing. No other days exist but these of ours before the tomb, both for us the waste them, not to waste anything of what I am, of what I could be: to do deeds helpful to the Frankish cause: to embrace, to be embraced by, proud Bradamante. I hope you spent your days no worse, oh corpse. Anyway to you the dice have already shown their numbers. For me they are still whirling in the box. And I love my own disquiet, corpse, not your peace.'

Agilulf is mistaken, in that he *does* have an attitude all his own, while Gurduloo is even more off-the-point, since he is simply unaware of his separate existence. Only Raimbaud is accurate, in love with his own disquiet, which is life itself. He is fit husband for Bradamante, who closes the book as she hurries to meet him, forsaking her other identity as Sister Theodora, the narrative voice. She cries out to the future, in a comic ecstasy:

What unforseeable golden ages art thou preparing, ill-mastered, indomitable harbinger of treasures dearly paid for, my kingdom to be conquered, the future ...

Flannery O'Connor

(1925–1964)

A PROFESSEDLY ROMAN CATHOLIC PROSE ROMANCE BEGINS WITH THE death of an eighty-four-year-old Southern American Protestant, self-called prophet, and professional moonshiner, as set forth in this splendidly comprehensive sentence:

> Francis Marion Tarwater's uncle had been dead for only half a day when the boy got too drunk to finish digging his grave and a Negro named Buford Munson, who had come to get a jug filled, had to finish it and drag the body from the breakfast table where it was still sitting and bury it in a decent and Christian way, with the sign of its Saviour at the head of the grave and enough dirt on top to keep the dogs from digging it up.

Flannery O'Connor's masterwork, *The Violent Bear It Away*, ends with the fourteen-year-old Tarwater marching towards the city of destruction, where his own career as prophet is to be suffered:

> Intermittently the boy's jagged shadow slanted across the road ahead of him as if it cleared a rough path toward his goal. His singed eyes, black in their deep sockets, seemed already to envision the fate that awaited him but he moved steadily on, his face set toward the dark city, where the children of God lay sleeping.

In Flannery O'Connor's fierce vision, the children of God, all of us, always are asleep in the outward life. Young Tarwater, clearly O'Connor's surrogate, is in clinical terms a borderline schizophrenic, subject to auditory hallucinations in which he hears the advice of an imaginary friend who is overtly the Christian Devil. But clinical terms are utterly alien to O'Connor, who accepts only theological namings and unnamings. This is necessarily a spiritual strength in O'Connor, yet it can be an aesthetic distraction also, since *The Violent Bear It Away* is a fiction of preternatural power, and not a religious tract. Rayber, the antagonist of both prophets, old and young Tarwater, is an aesthetic disaster, whose defects in representation alone keep the book from making a strong third with Faulkner's *As I Lay Dying* and Nathanael West's *Miss Lonelyhearts*. O'Connor despises Rayber, and cannot bother to make him even minimally persuasive. We wince at his unlikely verbal mixture of popular sociology and confused psychology, as even Sally Fitzgerald, O'Connor's partisan, is compelled to admit:

> Her weaknesses—a lack of perfect familiarity with the terminology of the secular sociologists, psychologists, and rationalists she often casts as adversary figures, and an evident weighting of the scales against them all—are present in the character of Rayber (who combines all three categories).

One hardly believes that a perfect familiarity with the writings say of David Riesman, Erik Erikson, and Karl Popper would have enabled O'Connor to make poor Rayber a more plausible caricature of what she despised. We remember *The Violent Bear It Away* for its two prophets, and particularly young Tarwater, who might be called a Gnostic version of Huckleberry Finn. What makes us free is the Gnosis, according to the most ancient of heresies. O'Connor, who insisted upon her Catholic orthodoxy, necessarily believed that what makes us free is baptism in Christ, and for her the title of her novel was its most important aspect, since the words are spoken by Jesus himself:

> But what went ye out for to see? A prophet? yea, I say unto you, and more than a prophet.
>
> For this is *he*, of whom it is written, Behold, I send my messenger before thy face, which shall prepare thy way before thee.
>
> Verily I say unto you, Among them that are born of women there hath not risen a greater than John the Baptist: notwithstanding he that is least in the kingdom of heaven is greater than he.
>
> And from the days of John the Baptist until now the kingdom of heaven suffereth violence, and the violent take it by force.

I have quoted the King James Version of Matt. 11:9–12, where "and the violent take it by force" is a touch more revealing than O'Connor's Catholic version, "and the violent bear it away." For O'Connor, we are back in or rather never have left Christ's time of urgency, and her heart is with those like the Tarwaters who know that the kingdom of heaven will suffer them to take it by force:

> The lack of realism would be crucial if this were a realistic novel or if the novel demanded the kind of realism you demand. I don't believe it does. The old man is very obviously not a Southern Baptist, but an independent, a prophet in the true sense. The true prophet is inspired by the Holy Ghost, not necessarily by the dominant religion of his region. Further, the traditional Protestant bodies of the South are evaporating into secularism and respectability and are being replaced on the grass roots level by all sorts of strange sects that bear not much resemblance to traditional Protestantism—Jehovah's Witnesses, snake-handlers, Free Thinking Christians, Independent Prophets, the swindlers, the mad, and sometimes the genuinely inspired. A character has to be true to his own nature and I think the old man is that. He was a prophet, not a church-member. As a prophet, he has to be a natural Catholic. Hawthorne said he didn't write novels, he wrote romances; I am one of his descendants.

O'Connor's only disputable remark in this splendid defense of her book is the naming of old Tarwater as "a natural Catholic." Hawthorne's descendant she certainly was, by way of Faulkner, T.S. Eliot, and Nathanael West, but though Hawthorne would have approved her mode, he would have been shocked by her matter. To ignore what is authentically shocking about O'Connor is to misread her weakly. It is not her incessant violence that is troublesome but rather her passionate endorsement of that violence as the only way to startle her secular readers into a spiritual awareness. As a visionary writer, she is determined to take us by force, to bear us away so that we may be open to the possibility of grace. Her unbelieving reader is represented by the grandmother in the famous story "A Good Man Is Hard to Find":

> She saw the man's face twisted close to her own as if he were going to cry and she murmured, "Why you're one of my babies. You're one of my own children!" She reached out and touched him on the shoulder. The Misfit sprang back as if a

snake had bitten him and shot her three times through the chest. Then he put his gun down on the ground and took off his glasses and began to clean them.

That murmur of recognition is what matters for O'Connor. The Misfit speaks for her in his mordant observation: "She would of been a good woman, if it had been somebody there to shoot her every minute of her life." Secular critic as I am, I need to murmur: "Surely that does make goodness a touch too strenuous?" But O'Connor anticipates our wounded outcries of nature against grace, since we understandably prefer a vision that corrects nature without abolishing it. Young Tarwater himself, as finely recalcitrant a youth as Huckleberry Finn, resists not only Rayber but the tuition of old Tarwater. A kind of swamp fox, like the Revolutionary hero for whom he was named, the boy Tarwater waits for his own call, and accepts his own prophetic election only after he has baptized his idiot cousin Bishop by drowning him, and even then only in consequence of having suffered a homosexual rape by the Devil himself. O'Connor's audacity reminds us of the Faulkner of *Sanctuary* and the West of *A Cool Million*. Her theology purports to be Roman Catholicism, but her sensibility is Southern Gothic, Jacobean in the mode of the early T.S. Eliot, and even Gnostic, in the rough manner of Carlyle, a writer she is likely never to have read.

I myself find it a critical puzzle to read her two novels, *Wise Blood* and *The Violent Bear It Away*, and her two books of stories, *A Good Man Is Hard to Find* and *Everything That Rises Must Converge*, and then to turn from her fiction to her occasional prose in *Mystery and Manners*, and her letters in *The Habit of Being*. The essayist and letter-writer denounces Manichaeism, Jansenism, and all other deviations from normative Roman Catholicism, while the storyteller seems a curious blend of the ideologies of Simone Weil reading the New Testament into the *Iliad*'s "poem of force" and of René Girard assuring us that there can be no return of the sacred without violence. Yet the actual O'Connor, in her letters, found Weil "comic and terrible," portraying the perpetual waiter for grace as an "angular intellectual proud woman approaching God inch by inch with ground teeth," and I suspect she would have been as funny about the violent thematicism of Girard.

To find something of a gap between O'Connor as lay theologue and O'Connor as a storyteller verging upon greatness may or may not be accurate but in any case intends to undervalue neither the belief nor the fiction. I suspect though that the fiction's implicit theology is very different from what O'Connor thought it to be, a difference that actually enhances the power of the novels and stories. It is not accidental that *As I Lay Dying* and *Miss Lonelyhearts* were the only works of fiction that O'Connor urged upon Robert Fitzgerald, or that her own prose cadences were haunted always by the earlier rather than the later Eliot. *The Waste Land*, *As I Lay Dying*, and *Miss Lonelyhearts* are not works of the Catholic imagination but rather of that Gnostic pattern Gershom Scholem termed "redemption through sin." *Wise Blood*, *The Violent Bear It Away*, and stories like "A Good Man Is Hard to Find" and the merciless "Parker's Back," take place in the same cosmos as *The Waste Land*, *As I Lay Dying*, and *Miss Lonelyhearts*. This world is the American version of the cosmological emptiness that the ancient Gnostics called the *kenoma*, a sphere ruled by a demiurge who has usurped the alien God, and who has exiled God out of history and beyond the reach of our prayers.

II

In recognizing O'Connor's fictive universe as being essentially Gnostic, I dissent not only from her own repudiation of heresy but from the sensitive reading of Jefferson Humphries, who links O'Connor to Proust in an "aesthetic of violence":

> For O'Connor, man has been his own demiurge, the author of his own fall, the keeper of his own cell....
> The chief consequence of this partly willful, partly inherited alienation from the sacred is that the sacred can only intrude upon human perception as a violence, a rending of the fabric of daily life.

On this account, which remains normative, whether Hebraic or Catholic, we are fallen into the *kenoma* through our own culpability. In the Gnostic formulation, creation and fall were one and the same event, and all that can save us is a certain spark within us, a spark that is no part of the creation but rather goes back to the original abyss. The grandeur or sublimity that shines through the ruined creation is a kind of abyss-radiance, whether in Blake or Carlyle or the early Eliot or in such novelistic masters of the grotesque as Faulkner, West, and O'Connor.

The ugliest of O'Connor's stories, yet one of the strongest, is "A View of the Woods" in *Everything That Rises Must Converge*. Its central characters are the seventy-nine-year-old Mr. Fortune, and his nine-year-old granddaughter, Mary Fortune Pitts. I am uncertain which of the two is the more abominable moral character or hideous human personality, partly because they resemble one another so closely in selfishness, obdura-cy, false pride, sullenness, and just plain meanness. At the story's close, a physical battle between the two leaves the little girl a corpse, throttled and with her head smashed upon a rock, while her grandfather suffers a heart attack, during which he has his final "view of the woods," in one of O'Connor's typically devastating final paragraphs:

> Then he fell on his back and looked up helplessly along the bare trunks into the tops of the pines and his heart expanded once more with a convulsive motion. It expanded so fast that the old man felt as if he were being pulled after it through the woods, felt as if he were running as fast as he could with the ugly pines toward the lake. He perceived that there would be a little open-ing there, a little place where he could escape and leave the woods behind him. He could see it in the distance already, a lit-tle opening where the white sky was reflected in the water. It grew as he ran toward it until suddenly the whole lake opened up before him, riding majestically in little corrugated folds toward his feet. He realized suddenly that he could not swim and that he had not bought the boat. On both sides of him he saw that the gaunt trees had thickened into mysterious dark files that were marching across the water and away into the distance. He looked around desperately for someone to help him but the place was deserted except for one huge yellow monster which sat to the side, as stationary as he was, gorging itself on clay.

The huge yellow monster is a bulldozer, and so is the dying Mr. Fortune, and so was the dead Mary Fortune Pitts. What sustains our inter-est in such antipathetic figures in so grossly unsympathetic a world? O'Connor's own commentary does not help answer the question, and introduces a bafflement quite its own:

> The woods, if anything, are the Christ symbol. They walk across the water, they are bathed in a red light, and they in the end escape the old man's vision and march off over the hills. The name of the story is a view of the woods and the woods alone are pure enough to be a Christ symbol if anything is. Part of the tension of the story is created by Mary Fortune and the old man being images of each other but opposite in the end. One is saved and the other is dammed [*sic*] and there is no way out of it, it must be pointed out and underlined. Their fates are

different. One has to die first because one kills the other, but you have read it wrong if you think they die in different places. The old man dies by her side; he only thinks he runs to the edge of the lake, that is his vision.

What divine morality it can be that saves May Fortune and damns her wretched grandfather is beyond my ken, but the peculiarities of O'Connor's sense of the four last things transcend me at all times, anyway. What is more interesting is O'Connor's own final view of the woods. Her sacramental vision enables her to see Christ in "the gaunt trees [that] had thickened into mysterious dark files that were marching across the water and away into the distance." Presumably their marching away is emblematic of Mr. Fortune's damnation, so far as O'Connor is concerned. As a reader of herself, I cannot rank O'Connor very high here. Surely Mary Fortune is as damnable and damned as her grandfather, and the woods are damnable and damned also. They resemble not the normative Christ but the Jesus of the Gnostic texts, whose phantom only suffers upon the cross while the true Christ laughs far off in the alien heavens, in the ultimate abyss.

O'Connor's final visions are more equivocal than she evidently intended. Here is the conclusion of "Revelation":

> Until the sun slipped finally behind the tree line, Mrs. Turpin remained there with her gaze bent to them as if she were absorbing some abysmal life-giving knowledge. At last she lifted her head. There was only a purple streak in the sky, cutting through a field of crimson and leading, like an extension of the highway, into the descending dusk. She raised her hands from the side of the pen in a gesture hieratic and profound. A visionary light settled in her eyes. She saw the streak as a vast swinging bridge extending upward from the earth through a field of living fire. Upon it a vast horde of souls were rumbling toward heaven. There were whole companies of white-trash, clean for the first time in their lives, and bands of black niggers in white robes, and battalions of freaks and lunatics shouting and clapping and leaping like frogs. And bringing up the end of the procession was a tribe of people whom she recognized at once as those who, like herself and Claud, had always had a little of everything and the God-given wit to use it right. She leaned forward to observe them closer. They were marching behind the others with great dignity, accountable as they had always been for good order and common sense and respectable

behavior. They alone were on key. Yet she could see by their shocked and altered faces that even their virtues were being burned away. She lowered her hands and gripped the rail of the hog pen, her eyes small but fixed unblinkingly on what lay ahead. In a moment the vision faded but she remained where she was, immobile.

At length she got down and turned off the faucet and made her slow way on the darkening path to the house. In the woods around her the invisible cricket choruses had struck up, but what she heard were the voices of the souls climbing upward into the starry field and shouting hallelujah.

This is meant to burn away false or apparent virtues, and yet consumes not less than everything. In O'Connor's mixed realm, which is neither nature nor grace, Southern reality nor private phantasmagoria, all are necessarily damned, not by an aesthetic of violence but by a Gnostic aesthetic in which there is no knowing unless the knower becomes one with the known. Her Catholic moralism masked from O'Connor something of her own aesthetic of the grotesque. Certainly her essay on "Some Aspects of the Grotesque in Southern Fiction" evades what is central in her own praxis:

> Whenever I'm asked why Southern writers particularly have a penchant for writing about freaks, I say it is because we are still able to recognize one. To be able to recognize a freak, you have to have some conception of the whole man, and in the South the general conception of man is still, in the main, theological. That is a large statement, and it is dangerous to make it, for almost anything you say about Southern belief can be denied in the next breath with equal propriety. But approaching the subject from the standpoint of the writer, I think it is safe to say that while the South is hardly Christ-centered, it is most certainly Christ-haunted. The Southerner, who isn't convinced of it, is very much afraid that he may have been formed in the image and likeness of God. Ghosts can be very fierce and instructive. They cast strange shadows, particularly in our literature. In any case, it is when the freak can be sensed as a figure for our essential displacement that he attains some depth in literature.

The freakish displacement here is from "wholeness," which is then described as the state of having been made in the image or likeness of God.

But that mode, displacement, is not what is operative in O'Connor's fiction. Her own favorite, among her people, is young Tarwater, who is not a freak, and who is so likeable because he values his own freedom above everything and anyone, even his call as a prophet. We are moved by Tarwater because of his recalcitrance, because he is the Huck Finn of visionaries. But he moves O'Connor, even to identification, because of his inescapable prophetic vocation. It is the interplay between Tarwater fighting to be humanly free, and Tarwater besieged by his great-uncle's training, by the internalized Devil, and most of all by O'Connor's own ferocious religious zeal, that constitutes O'Connor's extraordinary artistry. Her pious admirers to the contrary, O'Connor would have bequeathed us even stronger novels and stories, of the eminence of Faulkner's, if she had been able to restrain her spiritual tendentiousness.

Cynthia Ozick

(1928-)

"THE RECOVERY OF COVENANT CAN BE ATTAINED ONLY IN THE LIVING-OUT of the living Covenant; never among the shamanistic toys of literature." Such a sentence, typical of Cynthia Ozick's critical speculations, is fortunately contradicted by her narrative art. The author of "Envy; or, Yiddish in America" and of "Usurpation (Other People's Stories)," two novellas unequalled in her own generation, has recovered her version of Covenant among the tropes (or "shamanistic toys") of literature. Doubtless she lives out her own trust in a living Covenant also, since she is an authentic sharer in the normative tradition that, above all others in the West, bids us honor our mothers and our fathers, and more precisely, honor their virtues. But Ozick is neither a theologian, nor a literary critic, nor a Jewish historian. She does not deign to begin with a consciousness of rupture between normative Hebraism and her own vision. So decisive a denial of rupture must be honored as the given of her fiction, even as the fierce Catholicism of Flannery O'Connor must be accepted as the ground from which everything rises and converges in the author of *The Violent Bear It Away*.

Ozick's true precursor as a writer is Bernard Malamud, who hovers rather uneasily close in stories like "The Pagan Rabbi" and "The Dock-Witch," but who is triumphantly absorbed and transformed in Ozick's stronger works, including "Usurpation (Other People's Stories)." "Usurpation" is Ozick's central story, the key signature of her quest as a writer, just as her most brilliant nonfictional prose (except for the poignant "A Drugstore in Winter") is her "Preface" to *Bloodshed and Three Novellas* (1976), which essentially is an introduction to "Usurpation."

The "Preface" lists the other people's stories:

The tale called "The Magic Crown" in my story is a para-
phrase, except for a twist in its ending, of Malamud's "The
Silver Crown"; the account of the disappointed messiah is
Agnon's; and David Stern's "Agnon, A Story" is the mischie-
vous seed of my metamorphosis of the Nobel Prize Winner.

The enumeration of Malamud, Agnon, and Stern here is anything
but an indication of an anxiety. But then Ozick does confess what she
wishes us to believe is a literary anxiety, or perhaps rather a scruple or
reservation:

"These words." They are English words. I have no other language. Since my slave-ancestors left off building the Pyramids
to wander in the wilderness of Sinai, they have spoken a handful of generally obscure languages—Hebrew, Aramaic, twelfth-
century French perhaps, Yiddish for a thousand years. Since
the coming forth from Egypt five millennia ago, mine is the
first generation to think and speak and write wholly in English.
To say that I have been thoroughly assimilated into English
would of course be the grossest understatement—what is the
English language (and its poetry) if not my passion, my blood,
my life? But that perhaps is overstatement. A language while
we are zealously acquiring it can become a passion and a life. A
language owned in the root of the tongue is loved without
being the object of love: there is no sense of separateness from
it. Do I love my eyeballs? No; but sight is everything.
    Still, though English is my everything, now and then I feel
cramped by it. I have come to it with notions it is too parochial
to recognize. A language, like a people, has a history of ideas;
but not all ideas; only those known to its experience. Not surprisingly, English is a Christian language. When I write
English, I live in Christendom.

Ozick ostensibly defends herself from a nameless critic who evidently was not antithetical enough to understand her sense of the agonistic element in her writing. She goes so far as to add: "I had written 'Usurpation'
in the language of a civilization that cannot imagine its thesis." This is eloquent, but her perspective is a touch foreshortened, and nowhere more
than when she writes: "the theme that obsesses my tale ... the worry is this:
whether Jews ought to be storytellers. Conceive of Chaucer fretting over
whether Englishmen should be storytellers!"

Well, here *is* Chaucer, more than fretting over whether the Englishman Chaucer should be a storyteller:

> For our Book says "All that is written is for our doctrine" and that is my intention. Wherefore I beseech you meekly, for the mercy of God, that you pray for me that Christ have mercy on me and forgive me my guilts and namely of my translations and editings of worldly vanities, that which I revoke in my retractions.
> [modernized]

With this as prelude, Chaucer proceeds to retract *Troilus* and *The Canterbury Tales*. Supposedly that is Chaucer on his deathbed, but at the close of *Troilus* itself he says much the same. The conflict or anxiety Ozick describes is at least as much Christian as it is Jewish, and the English language she calls Christian is no more Christian than it is Jewish or Buddhist. Like all language, it is steeped in anterior images, and any wresting of a strong new achievement from it must be what Ozick accurately calls a "usurpation" of an old story by a new one, whether the storyteller be Christian or Jewish. All belated stories, and not just her "Usurpation," are in one sense written, as she says, "against story-writing," as all belated poems are written against poetry and even against poem-making. The phenomenon Ozick addresses with great vigor and freshness is a very old phenomenon, as old as Hellenistic Alexandria, home of the first of the many recurrent literary "modernisms."

Ozick's concern, that is to say, is critically as old as Alexandria, Gentile *and* Jewish, and religiously as old as Gnosticism, again Gentile *and* Jewish, as Gershom Scholem massively demonstrated. In "Usurpation," Ozick has Agnon appropriately denounce Gnosticism, but she herself, as a storyteller, not as a Jew, is certainly just as Gnostic as Kafka or as Balzac. As she remarks, she lusts after forbidden or Jewish magic. This is why she is preoccupied with the troublesome Kabbalistic *Keter* or silver crown that is her peculiar twist or trope away from Malamud in "Usurpation." Thus she makes Agnon say: "When a writer wishes to usurp the place and power of another writer, he simply puts it on." As Ozick triumphantly shows, that "simply" is madly dialectical. Very powerfully, she has the ghost of the great modern Hebrew poet, the paganizing Tchernikhovsky, say: "In Eden there's nothing but lust," where "lust" is a comprehensive metaphor that includes the ambition that makes for agonistic strivings between writers. These are indeed what Blake called the wars of Eden, the Mental Fight that constitutes Eternity.

Ozick's most profound insight into her own ambivalence in this area is a superb starting point for the Gnosis she condemns as the religion of art, or worship of Moloch, and is manifested when she asks herself the agonistic question that governs the incarnation of every strong writer: "Why do we become what we most desire to contend with?" Her immensely bitter reply is made in the closing paragraph of "Usurpation (Other People's Stories)":

> Only Tchernikhovsky and the shy old writer of Jerusalem have ascended. The old writer of Jerusalem is a fiction; murmuring psalms, he snacks on leviathan and polishes his Prize with the cuff of his sleeve. Tchernikhovsky eats nude at the table of the nude gods, clean-shaven now, his limbs radiant, his youth restored, his sex splendidly erect, the discs of his white ears sparkling, a convivial fellow; he eats without self-restraint from the celestial menu, and when the Sabbath comes (the Sabbath of Sabbaths, which flowers every seven centuries in the perpetual Sabbath of Eden), as usual he avoids the congregation of the faithful before the Footstool and the Throne. Then the taciturn little Canaanite idols call him, in the language of the spheres, kike.

It would be a more effective conclusion, I think, if the last sentence were omitted. But nothing is got for nothing, and Ozick's emotional directness remains one of her imaginative virtues, even if it sometimes renders her dialectical ironies less immediately effective.

II

Art & Ardor, Ozick's gathering of her essays, has a curiously mixed performance courageously entitled "Toward a New Yiddish." Its argument again exposes Ozick to a creative blindness concerning the sharing of precisely the same dilemmas by any literature aspiring to be either specifically Christian or specifically Jewish:

> By "centrally Jewish" I mean, for literature, whatever touches on the liturgical. Obviously this does not refer only to prayer. It refers to a type of literature and to a type of perception. There is a critical difference between liturgy and a poem. Liturgy is in command of the reciprocal moral imagination rather than of the isolated lyrical imagination. A poem is a private flattery: it moves the private heart, but to no end other

than being moved. A poem is a decoration of the heart, the art of the instant. It is what Yehudah Halevi called flowers without fruit. Liturgy is also a poem, but it is meant not to have only a private voice. Liturgy has a choral voice, a communal voice: the echo of the voice of the Lord of History. Poetry shuns judgment and memory and seizes the moment. In all of history the literature that has lasted for Jews has been liturgical. The secular Jew is a figment; when a Jew becomes a secular person he is no longer a Jew. This is especially true for makers of literature. It was not only an injunction that Moses uttered when he said we would be a people attentive to holiness: it was a description and a destiny.

It takes a kind of moral courage to say that, "Poetry shuns judgment and memory and seizes the moment," but I am distressed to hear Ozick sounding like W.H. Auden at *his* most self-deceived:

> The Incarnation, the coming of Christ in the form of a servant who cannot be recognized by the eye of flesh and blood, but only by the eye of faith, puts an end to all claims of the imagination to be the faculty which decides what is truly sacred and what is profane. A pagan god can appear on earth in disguise but, so long as he wears his disguise, no man is expected to recognize him nor can. But Christ appears looking just like any other man, yet claims that He is the Way, the Truth and the Life, and that no man can come to God the Father except through Him. The contradiction between the profane appearance and the sacred assertion is impassible to the imagination.

Ozick and Auden alike repeat T.S. Eliot's prime error, which was and is a failing to see that there are only political or societal distinctions between supposedly secular and supposedly sacred literatures. Secularization is never an imaginative process, whereas canonization is. Fictions remain stubbornly archaic and idolatrous, to the scandal of Eliot and Auden as pious Christians, and of Ozick as a pious Jew, but very much to the delight of Eliot and Auden as poets and dramatists, and of Ozick as story-writer and novelist. You do not defend yourself, or anyone else, from the archaic by writing a poem or a novella. Rather, instead of choosing a form of worship from a poetic tale, you attempt to write another poetic tale that can usurp its precursors' space, their claim upon our limited and waning attention. Devotional short stories are as dubious as devotional poems, despite say Flannery O'Connor's weird self-deception that her superbly brutal "A Good Man Is Hard to Find" was a Catholic narrative, or Ozick's equally strange conviction that the savage and sublime "Envy; or, Yiddish in America" somehow might become a contribution "Toward a New Yiddish," toward a survival that Ozick wistfully but wrongly identifies with Jewish liturgy.

Ozick, I would wish to emphasize, is all the stronger a writer for being so self-deceived a reader, including a misreader of the fictions of Cynthia Ozick. Denouncing the archaic, she slyly immerses herself in its destructive element, knowing as she does that her daemon tells the stories, while it cheerfully allows Ozick our rabbi and teacher to write the essays. I have just reread "Envy; or, Yiddish in America" for the twentieth or so time since its initial magazine appearance, and have found it as vital, crazily funny, and ultimately tragic a novella as it seemed to me in November 1969, more than sixteen years ago. If I live, I will find it as fresh and wise in 2009 as I do now. Nothing else since Isaac Babel in modern Jewish fiction challenges the Philip Roth of *The Anatomy Lesson* and "The Prague Orgy" as an instance of that peculiarly Jewish laughter that cleanses us even as it pains us. I remember always in particular the scene of mutual rejection between Edelshtein, untranslated poet, and young Hannah, who will not translate him:

> Edelshtein's hand, the cushiony underside of it, blazed from giving the blow. "You," he said, "you have no ideas, what are you?" A shred of learning flaked from him, what the sages said of Job ripped from his tongue like a peeling of the tongue itself, *he never was, he never existed.* "You were never born, you were never created!" he yelled. "Let me tell you, a dead man tells you this, at least I had a life, at least I understood something!"
>
> "Die," she told him. "Die now, all you old men, what are you waiting for? Hanging on my neck, him and now you, the whole bunch of you, parasites, hurry up and die."
>
> His palm burned, it was the first time he had ever slapped a child. He felt like a father. Her mouth lay back naked on her face. Out of spite, against instinct, she kept her hands from the bruise—he could see the shape of her teeth, turned a little one on the other, imperfect, again vulnerable. From fury her nose streamed. He had put a bulge in her lip.
>
> "Forget Yiddish!" he screamed at her. "Wipe it out of your brain! Extirpate it! Go get a memory operation! You have no

right to it, you have no right to an uncle, a grandfather! No one ever came before you, you were never born! A vacuum!"

"You old atheists," she called after him. "You dead old socialists. Boring! You bore me to death. You hate magic, you hate imagination, you talk God and you hate God, you despise, you bore, you envy, you eat people up with your disgusting old age—cannibals, all you care about is your own youth, you're finished, give somebody else a turn!"

As a dialogue between the generations, it hurts magnificently, with the immanent strength of a recurrent vision of reality. Ozick herself is on both sides and on neither, *as a storyteller*, and it is as storyteller that she presents us with Edelshtein's closing hysteria, when he shouts his whole self-violated being into a phone call to "Christ's Five-Day Inexpensive Elect-Plan," a call-service prefiguring the Moral Majority:

Edelshtein shouted into the telephone, "Amalekite! Titus! Nazi! The whole world is infected by you anti-Semites! On account of you children become corrupted! On account of you I lost everything, my whole life! On account of you I have no translator!"

The high comedy of this invective depends upon Edelshtein's not altogether pathetic insistence that he is an authentic representative of waning Yiddish culture. Like Malamud, Ozick captures both the humane pathos and the ironic ethos of Yiddish culture in its tragicomic predicament. In a mode that is now authentically her own, she trusts in the storyteller's only covenant, working to defer a future in which stories no longer could be told. This is not the Covenant she seeks to celebrate, but that does not disturb the aesthetic dignity of her best work. As person, she trusts in the Covenant between God and his people, Israel. As writer, she trusts the covenant between her stories and other people's stories, between her own strength of usurpation and the narrative tradition's power to both absorb and renew her.

John Updike

(1932–)

JOHN UPDIKE IS A MAJOR STYLIST, WHOSE LITERARY PRODUCTION HAS BEEN vast and varied. He may be most himself in his short stories, where style itself can constitute a mode of vision. No novel by Updike persuades me as fully as do stories like "A&P" and "Pigeon Feathers," if only because the novelist so overtly contaminates his principal longer narratives with his own beliefs and opinions. Frequently, these judgments and views are of considerable interest in themselves, but they can distract the reader's attention from persons, places, and events.

In "A&P" there are no distractions, and Updike's art is as subtle as Joyce's in *Dubliners*. Sammy, nineteen and very limited in education and social understanding, falls into a passion for "Queenie," a young beauty who never will be available to someone of his social class. He makes the Quixotic gesture of quitting his job at the A&P, though "Queenie" never will know that he has protested against her embarrassment by the store manager. Updike deftly conveys that Sammy's action is more a pose than a gesture, though Sammy says: "it seems to me that once you begin a gesture it's fatal not to go through with it."

The sad reality is that gestures are for those who can afford them, and Sammy cannot. Updike accurately can be praised for profound social insight in "A&P," but the story, like Joyce's "Two Gallants" or "Araby," is imaginatively richer than social understanding tends to be by itself. In less than half-a-dozen pages, Updike condenses a life, up to its nineteenth year, and also intimates how unlikely that life is to develop in any way that might satisfy its dream of erotic fulfillment. The economy of "A&P," and its consistent verbal rightness, testify to a superb artist in the short-story form.

Raymond Carver

(1938–1988)

I HAVE AN IMPERFECT SYMPATHY FOR RAYMOND CARVER'S STORIES, THOUGH I agree with such eminent critics as Frank Kermode and Irving Howe that Carver was a master within the limits he imposed upon himself. So overwhelming was Hemingway's influence upon Carver's earlier stories that the later writer wisely fended Hemingway off by an *askesis* that went well beyond the elliptical style practiced by the author of *The First Forty-Nine Stories*. In his own, final phase, Carver began to develop beyond an art so largely reliant upon leaving things out. "Cathedral" is my favorite story by Carver, but it involves the fully aware reader in some perplexity, because of its puzzling relationship to D.H. Lawrence's magnificent short story, "The Blind Man." It seems hardly possible that Carver did not know how much "Cathedral" owed to "The Blind Man," but literary influence is a labyrinth, and good writers can become remarkably schooled at repression, or unconsciously purposeful forgetting.

Keith Cushman first noted Carver's debt, which Cushman wittily termed "blind intertextuality." In Lawrence's story, the visiting friend who comes from afar can see; it is the husband who is blind. Carver's story is based upon a visit from a blind friend of Tess Gallagher's, and ends with an overcoming of the narrator's jealousy of the visitor:

> So we kept on with it. His fingers rode my fingers as my hand went over the paper. It was like nothing else in my life up to now.
>
> Then he said, "I think that's it. I think you got it," he said. "Take a look. What do you think?"
>
> But I had my eyes closed. I thought I'd keep them that way for a little longer. I thought it was something I ought to do.

"Well?" he said. "Are you looking?"

My eyes were still closed. I was in my house. I knew that. But I didn't feel like I was inside anything.

"It's really something," I said.

This poignant opening to otherness is overmatched by the parallel passage in Lawrence, when the blind husband establishes contact with the terrified visitor:

"Your head seems tender, as if you were young," Maurice repeated. "So do your hands. Touch my eyes, will you?—touch my scar."

Now Bertie quivered with revulsion. Yet he was under the power of the blind man, as if hypnotised. He lifted his hand, and laid the fingers on the scar, on the scarred eyes. Maurice suddenly covered them with his own hand, pressed the fingers of the other man upon his disfigured eye-sockets, trembling in every fibre, and rocking slightly, slowly, from side to side. He remained thus for a minute or more, whilst Bertie stood as if in a swoon, unconscious, imprisoned.

Then suddenly Maurice removed the hand of the other man from his brow, and stood holding it in his own.

"Oh, my God," he said, "we shall know each other now, shan't we? We shall know each other now."

Bertie could not answer. He gazed mute and terror-struck, overcome by his own weakness. He knew he could not answer. He had an unreasonable fear, lest the other man should suddenly destroy him. Whereas Maurice was actually filled with hot, poignant love, the passion of friendship. Perhaps it was this very passion of friendship which Bertie shrank from most.

"We're all right together now, aren't we?" said Maurice. "It's all right now, as long as we live, so far as we're concerned."

"Yes," said Bertie, trying by any means to escape.

This is scarcely a comparison that Carver can sustain, but then Lawrence is extraordinary in his short stories, fully the peer of Turgenev, Chekhov, Joyce, Isaac Babel, and Hemingway. Carver, whom perhaps we have over praised, died before he could realize the larger possibilities of his art. In "The Blind Man" there is a homoerotic element, but it is secondary. Blind Maurice is admitting Bertie to the interiority that is shared only with his wife, but Bertie cannot bear intimacy: he has been seared by the touch. There is a reverberation in Lawrence's story that carries us into the high madness of great art. Carver, though a very fine artist, cannot carry us there.

Further Reading

Allen, Walter. *The Short Story in English*. Oxford: Clarendon Press, 1981.

Aycock, Wendell M., ed. *The Teller and the Tale: Aspects of the Short Story*. Lubbock: Texas Tech Press, 1982.

Bates, H.E. *The Modern Short Story: A Critical Survey*, London: Joseph, 1972.

Beachcroft, Thomas O. *The English Short Story*. London: Longmans, Green, 1964.

———. *The Modest Art: A Survey of the Short Story in English*. London: Oxford University Press, 1968.

Beale, Robert Cecil. *The Development of the Short Story in the South*. Philadelphia: R. West, 1977.

Bloom, Harold. *How to Read and Why*. New York: Scribner, 2000.

Current-Garcia, Eugene, ed. *The American Short Story Before 1850: A Critical History*. Boston: Twayne, 1985.

Current-Garcia, Eugene and Walton R. Patrick. *What Is the Short Story?* Glenview: Scott, Foresman, 1974.

Dunn, Maggie and Ann Morris. *The Composite Novel: The Short Story Cycle in Transition*. Farmington Hills: The Gale Group, 1995.

Evans, Robert C., Barbara Wiedemann, and Anne C. Little. *Short Fiction: A Critical Companion*. West Cornwall: Locust Hill Press, 1997.

Flora, Joseph M., ed. *The English Short Story, 1880–1945: A Critical History*. Boston: Twayne, 1985.

Gerwig, George William. *The Art of the Short Story*. Philadelphia: R. West, 1977.

Goodman, Henry, ed. *Creating the Short Story*. New York: Harcourt, Brace & Co., 1929.

Hanson, Clare, ed. *Rereading the Short Story*. New York: St. Martin's Press, 1989.

———. *Short Stories and Short Fictions, 1880–1980*, New York: St. Martin's Press, 1985.

Iftekharrudin, Farhat, et. al., ed. *The Postmodern Short Story: Forms and Issues*. Westport: Praeger, 2003.

Levy, Andrew. *The Culture and Commerce of the American Short Story*. Cambridge: Cambridge University Press, 1993.

Mann, Susan Garland. *The Short Story Cycle: A Genre Companion and Reference Guide*. Westport: Greenwood Press, 1989.

Martin, Wendy. *The Art of the Short Story*. Boston: Houghton Mifflin, 2005.

Nagel, James. *The Contemporary American Short-Story Cycle: The Ethnic Resonance of Genre*. Baton Rouge: Louisiana State University Press, 2001.

O'Connor, Frank. *The Lonely Voice: A Study of the Short Story*. Hoboken: Melville House Publishing, 2004.

Orel, Harold. *The Victorian Short Story: Development and Triumph of a Literary Genre*. New York: Cambridge University Press, 1986.

Shaw, Valerie. *The Short Story: A Critical Introduction*. New York: Longman, 1983.

Voss, Arthur. *American Short Story: A Critical Survey*. Norman: University of Oklahoma Press, 1973.

Ward, A.C. *Aspects of the Modern Short Story: English and American*. Philadelphia: R. West, 1977.

Index

About the Author

HAROLD BLOOM is Sterling Professor of the Humanities at Yale University. He is the author of over 20 books, including *Shelley's Mythmaking* (1959), *The Visionary Company* (1961), *Blake's Apocalypse* (1963), *Yeats* (1970), *A Map of Misreading* (1975), *Kabbalah and Criticism* (1975), *Agon: Toward a Theory of Revisionism* (1982), *The American Religion* (1992), *The Western Canon* (1994), and *Omens of Millennium: The Gnosis of Angels, Dreams, and Resurrection* (1996). *The Anxiety of Influence* (1973) sets forth Professor Bloom's provocative theory of the literary relationships between the great writers and their predecessors. His most recent books include *Shakespeare: The Invention of the Human* (1998), a 1998 National Book Award finalist, *How to Read and Why* (2000), *Genius: A Mosaic of One Hundred Exemplary Creative Minds* (2002), *Hamlet: Poem Unlimited* (2003), and *Where Shall Wisdom be Found* (2004). In 1999, Professor Bloom received the prestigious American Academy of Arts and Letters Gold Medal for Criticism, and in 2002 he received the Catalonia International Prize.